MW00814004

Quicken® 2001

fast&easy®

Send Us Your Comments:

To comment on this book or any other PRIMA TECH title, visit our reader response page on the Web at **www.prima-tech.com/comments**.

How to Order:

For information on quantity discounts, contact the publisher: Prima Publishing, P.O. Box 1260BK, Rocklin, CA 95677-1260; (916) 787-7000. On your letterhead, include information concerning the intended use of the books and the number of books you want to purchase.

Quicken® 2001

fast&easy®

Coletta and Craig
Witherspoon

A DIVISION OF PRIMA PUBLISHING

© 2000 by Prima Publishing. All rights reserved. No part of this book may be reproduced or transmitted in any form or by any means, electronic or mechanical, including photocopying, recording, or by any information storage or retrieval system without written permission from Prima Publishing, except for the inclusion of brief quotations in a review.

 A Division of Prima Publishing

Prima Publishing and colophon and Fast & Easy are registered trademarks of Prima Communications, Inc. PRIMA TECH is a trademark of Prima Communications, Inc., Roseville, California 95661.

Publisher: Stacy L. Hiquet
Marketing Manager: Judi Taylor
Associate Marketing Manager: Heather Buzzingham
Managing Editor: Sandy Doell
Acquisitions Editor: Emi Nakamura
Project Editor: Cathleen D. Snyder
Technical Reviewer: Diana Trabel
Copy Editor: Laura R. Gabler
Interior Layout: Shawn Morningstar
Cover Design: Prima Design Team
Indexer: Katherine Stimson

Intuit, Quicken, and EasyStep are registered trademarks and/or registered service marks of Intuit Inc. Billminder, Quicken.com, QuickFill, QuickTabs, and Quicken Financial planner are trademarks and/or service marks of Intuit Inc. or one of its subsidiaries. Edmunds.com is a service mark of Edmunds.com Inc.

Important: Prima Publishing cannot provide software support. Please contact the appropriate software manufacturer's technical support line or Web site for assistance.

Prima Publishing and the author have attempted throughout this book to distinguish proprietary trademarks from descriptive terms by following the capitalization style used by the manufacturer.

Information contained in this book has been obtained by Prima Publishing from sources believed to be reliable. However, because of the possibility of human or mechanical error by our sources, Prima Publishing, or others, the Publisher does not guarantee the accuracy, adequacy, or completeness of any information and is not responsible for any errors or omissions or the results obtained from use of such information. Readers should be particularly aware of the fact that the Internet is an ever-changing entity. Some facts may have changed since this book went to press.

ISBN: 0-7615-2908-x
Library of Congress Catalog Card Number: 00-107333
Printed in the United States of America

00 01 02 03 04 DD 10 9 8 7 6 5 4 3 2 1

To Dahlia and the Class of 2001

The hardest part of realizing your opportunities may be simply getting started. Once you decide what you want to do with your life, the adventure begins. You can meet the challenge. Determine the steps you must take along your path. But remember, nothing will happen unless you make it happen. Get up out of the chair, turn off the TV, and get going. Open a book and see what it says. Open your mind and see what you can put into it. Your life can be full of opportunity and excitement. The choice is up to you.

Acknowledgments

We want to express our thanks to everyone at Prima Publishing for the support and assistance we received throughout this entire book project. In particular, we would like to thank Emi Nakamura and Cathleen Snyder for making this a fun project.

About the Authors

COLETTA AND CRAIG WITHERSPOON are freelance writers who have authored twenty books about software applications, Internet tools, operating systems, networks, and networking tools.

Contents at a Glance

Contents

Introduction

This *Fast & Easy* guide from Prima Publishing will help you master Quicken Deluxe 2001 so that you can take charge of your personal finances. Quicken Deluxe 2001 is a popular financial management program that provides a complete and easy way to keep track of your financial records. Quicken has been popular with users for many years, and with each new version of the software, new features and abilities have been added. This makes Quicken easier to use, and it also means that even more information is available to help you make intelligent decisions about your finances.

Quicken Deluxe 2001 is a comprehensive financial management program that makes it easy to maintain checking and savings accounts, investment accounts, and inventories of your belongings. It also contains tools that calculate your financial outlook and help you plan for future events.

Whether you want to keep track of your checkbook or plan for a college education, you'll find the information you need in this book.

Who Should Read This Book?

This book is directed toward the novice computer user who needs a hands-on approach. Every step in this book is accompanied by an illustration of what you will see on your computer screen. You can follow along and check your results easily. The generous use of illustrations makes this an ideal tool for those who have never used a financial management program. This book is also for those who are familiar with previous versions of Quicken and are upgrading to Quicken Deluxe 2001.

This book is organized so that you can quickly look up tasks to complete a job or learn a new trick. You may need to read an entire chapter to master a subject, or you may need only to review a certain section of a chapter.

Added Advice to Make You a Financial Wizard

You'll notice that this book keeps explanations to a minimum to help you learn faster. Other features in this book provide more information on how to work with Quicken Deluxe 2001.

- **Tips** offer helpful hints about Quicken that make your job a little easier and help you manage your finances more efficiently.
- **Notes** offer additional information about Quicken to enhance your learning experience with the software.

The first appendix shows how to install Quicken Deluxe 2001 on your computer and the second appendix lists some of the keyboard shortcuts that can be used with Quicken if you are looking to reduce your mouse usage.

Enjoy!

PART I

Getting Organized

1

Learning about Quicken

Your adventure with Quicken 2001 is about to begin. Quicken is an easy-to-use financial management program that not only helps you keep your checkbook balanced, but also helps you track your investments and plan for the future. Before you get started on the road to financial prosperity, take some time to get familiar with the program and learn the ropes. There's a wealth of information inside Quicken to help you use the program and manage your finances. In this chapter, you'll learn how to:

- Open and close Quicken
- Set up your checking account in Quicken
- Become efficient with the program by using the Help files

Starting Quicken for the First Time

Once Quicken is installed on your computer, you'll notice that items have been added to the Windows Start menu and to the desktop. This is your gateway to the Quicken world. If this is your first time using Quicken, you'll also need to set up an account (such as your checking account) before you can begin using the program.

This book assumes you are using Quicken 2001 Deluxe. If you are using another version of Quicken, such as Quicken Home & Business, select the appropriate version when working through the examples in this chapter.

NOTE

If you need help installing Quicken, turn to Appendix A, "Installing and Upgrading Quicken."

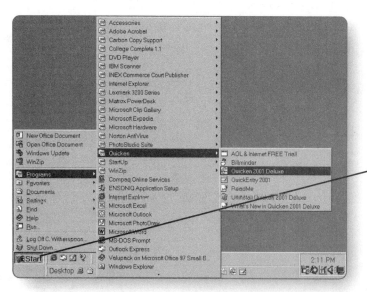

Opening Quicken

Like other Windows programs, Quicken can be accessed from the Start button or by clicking on the icon that Quicken adds to your desktop.

1. Click on the **Start button**. The Start menu will appear.

2. **Move** the **mouse pointer** to Programs. The Programs menu will appear.

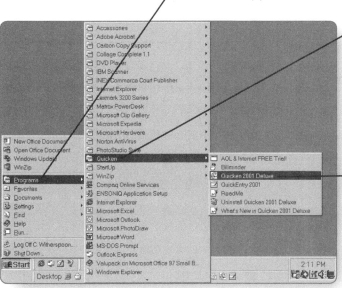

3. **Move** the **mouse pointer** to Quicken. The Quicken menu will appear. This menu contains some additional items that you may want to explore (such as the ReadMe and What's New in Quicken 2001 Deluxe).

4. **Click** on **Quicken 2001 Deluxe**. The Quicken program will open and the Quicken New User Setup wizard will begin.

NOTE

You may be asked if you want to register your copy of Quicken. If you do not want to register now, you can register your copy of the software later by opening the Help menu and selecting the Register Quicken menu item. The program will also give you a friendly reminder from time to time.

Setting Up a Bank Account

The first time you use Quicken, the Quicken New User Setup wizard will start. This wizard needs some basic information about you and how you'll be using Quicken. It uses this information to customize the program to fit your needs. Use the wizard to set up your first bank account. You can set up either a checking or a savings account. In the example that follows, you will set up a checking account.

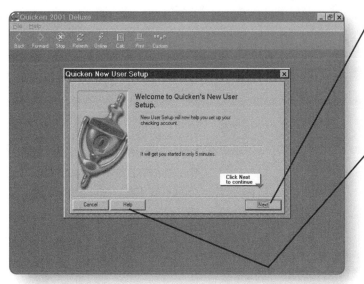

1. Click on **Next**. The Please tell Quicken about yourself screen will appear.

TIP

If you need help with any of the screens in the wizard, just click on the Help button. A window will open that contains more information.

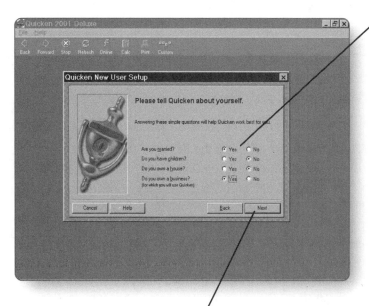

2. Click on the **Yes option button or the No option button** in response to each of the four questions. The option for each question will be selected.

NOTE

Your responses to these questions will help Quicken set up categories that you can use to track what you spend. You'll learn more about categories in Chapter 4, "Creating a Chart of Accounts."

3. Click on **Next**. The Let's set up your checking account screen will appear.

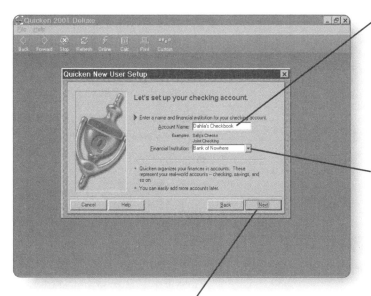

4. **Type** a **name** to identify the checking account in the Account Name text box. You might want to use the name of your bank or maybe the purpose of the checking account (such as Dahlia's First Checking Account).

5. **Click** on the **Financial Institution down arrow** and **select** your **bank** from the list. If your bank is not listed, you can type the name of your bank in the text box.

6. **Click** on **Next**. The Use your last bank statement as a starting point screen will appear.

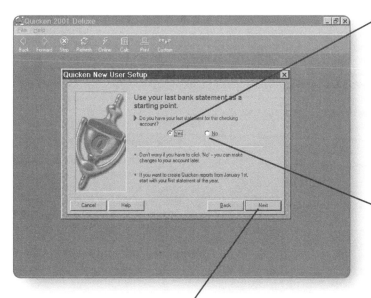

7a. **Click** on the **Yes option button** if you want to enter a beginning balance for your checking account. Use the bank statement that ends just prior to the date of the first transaction you enter into Quicken. The option will be selected.

OR

7b. **Click** on the **No option button** if you don't want to give Quicken a bank balance with which to start. The option will be selected.

8. **Click** on **Next**. The Enter the ending date and balance from your bank statement screen will appear if you selected the Yes option button (in Step 7a). If you selected the No option button (in Step 7b), proceed to Step 15.

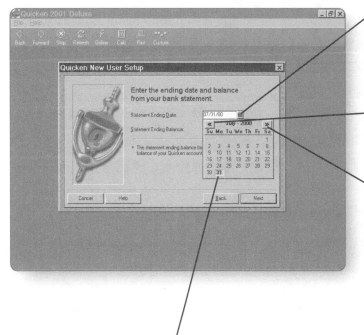

9. **Click** on the **Calendar icon** to the right of the Statement Ending Date text box. A calendar will appear.

10a. **Click** on the **Back button**. The previous month will appear.

OR

10b. **Click** on the **Forward button**. The next month will appear.

11. **Click** on the **Back or Forward button** until the month that corresponds to the ending date on the bank statement is displayed in the calendar.

12. **Click** on the **date** that corresponds to the ending date on the bank statement. The number will be selected, the calendar will disappear, and the ending date of the bank statement will appear in the Statement Ending Date text box.

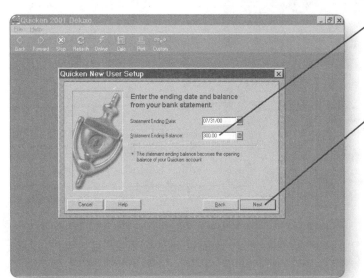

13. **Type** the **ending balance** from the bank statement in the Statement Ending Balance text box.

14. **Click** on **Next**. The You've just completed New User Setup screen will appear.

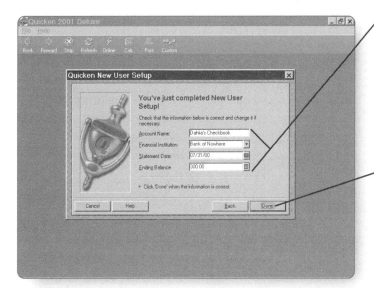

All the information that you entered into the wizard will appear in the four text boxes. You'll want to make sure that the information is correct. If not, you can make any corrections in these text boxes.

15. Click on **Done**. The Quicken program window will appear and you can begin to explore Quicken.

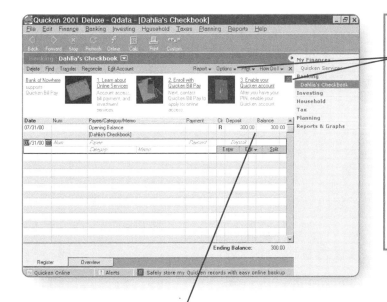

TIP

To make more space in the register, click on the Close button (☒) in the online services information area. If you want to display the online services information area, click on the Options button down arrow (▾) and select View Online Setup from the menu that appears.

Quicken will open and display the account register for the checking account you just created. If you set up the account with a beginning balance, you'll see that a transaction has been created for the opening balance. The register is also ready for you to enter your first transaction for this account.

Finding Help

Whether you're new to Quicken or you're using a feature for the first time, you may need some extra help using the program. Spending some time browsing the help tools will allow you to gain greater control over your finances and plan for future events. Besides the manual, Quicken comes equipped with quite an arsenal of help tools.

Reading the Help Book

As you might already know, most Windows programs include a help system that is accessible from the Help menu. These help files are organized in a book format that you can read from start to finish, or you can skip around and find information that pertains to the type of help you need.

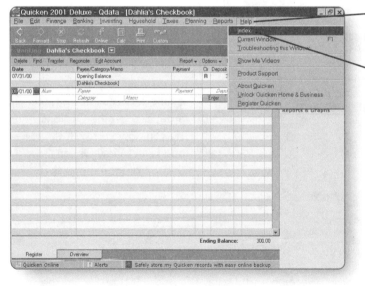

1. Click on **Help**. The Help menu will appear.

2. Click on **Index**. The Help Topics dialog box will open with the Index tab at the top of the stack.

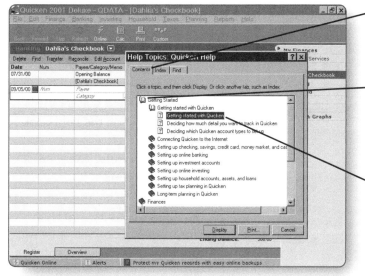

3. Click on the **Contents tab**. The Contents tab will move to the top of the stack.

4. Double-click on the **book icon** next to a topic. The topic will expand to show the contents.

5. Double-click on a **help topic**. The associated help file will appear in a separate window.

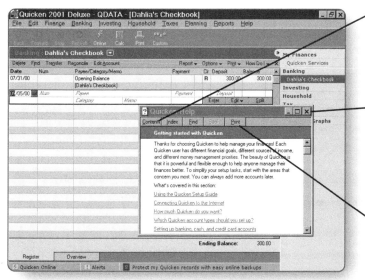

6a. Click on the **Contents button** to return to the Help Topics dialog box.

OR

6b. Click on the **Close button**. The help topic window and the Help Topics dialog box will close.

TIP

To keep a paper copy of a help topic, click on the Print button.

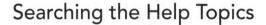

Searching the Help Topics

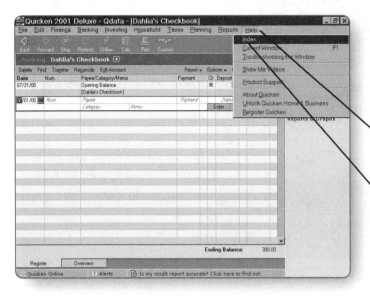

Another way to find help information is to search for a specific word or phrase. You may find this method quicker than reading through the help book.

1. Click on **Help**. The Help menu will appear.

2. Click on **Index**. The Help Topics dialog box will open with the Index tab at the top of the stack.

3. Click on the **Find tab**. The Find tab will move to the top of the stack.

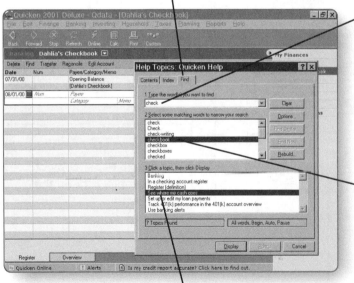

4. In the Type the word(s) you want to find text box, **type** a **word** that describes the information that you need. As you type, the list of matching words in the Select some matching words to narrow your search list box will be reduced.

5. Click on a **word** that better describes the information for which you are searching. A list of topics will appear in the Click a topic, then click Display list box.

6. Double-click on a **topic**. The associated help file will appear in a separate window.

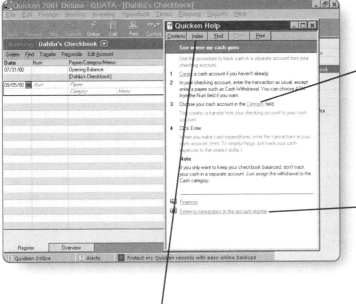

7. **Find** further **information** about the help topic by using one of the following methods.

- Click on text with a dotted underline to display a screen tip. These screen tips are usually a definition or an explanation of the underlined word. To close the screen tip, click outside of it.

- Click on text with a solid underline to go to a different help topic. Use the Back button to return to the previously viewed help topic.

8. Click on the **Index button**. You will return to the Help Topics dialog box and the Index tab will be at the top of the stack.

Getting More Help

In addition to the standard Windows help system, you'll also find quite a bit of additional help that is specific to the area within the Quicken program with which you are working. You'll find these sources of help useful while you are working in the Quicken program.

Going to the How Do I? Files

Every page in the Quicken program contains help that is specific to that particular page. If you have a question about how to work with the information presented on a page, you'll want to give this option a try. Clicking on a question in the How do I menu opens a Help dialog box that answers the selected question and gives further information about related topics.

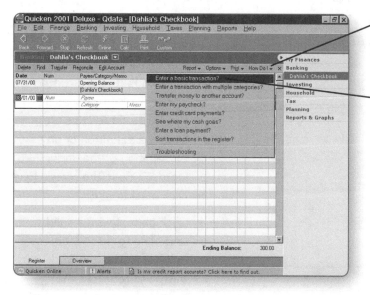

1. **Click** on the **How Do I button**. The How Do I menu will appear.

2. **Click** on the **question** that you would like answered. The Quicken Help window will open.

3. **Read** the **instructions** for performing the selected task.

4. **Click** on the **Close button** when you are finished. The Help window will close.

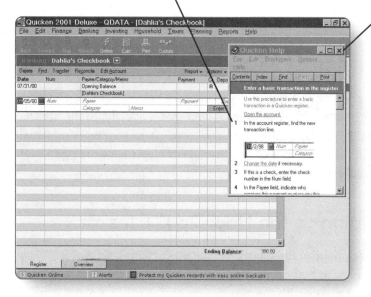

Getting Help on the Current Window

When you want to know more about the displayed Quicken program window, try this handy help tool.

1. Display the **window** with which you need help. The window will appear in the Quicken program.

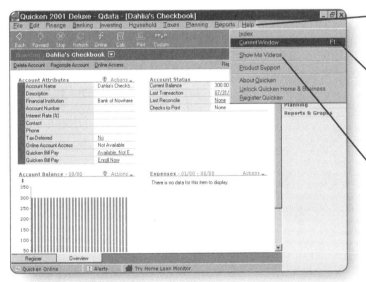

2. Click on **Help**. The Help menu will appear.

3. Click on **Current Window**. The Quicken Help window will open.

TIP

If you like watching movies, you can play the Show Me Videos to learn how to perform specific tasks. Before you can play the videos, you must set up Quicken to access the Internet. You'll learn how to use Quicken on the Internet in Chapter 2, "Exploring the Quicken World."

---

4. Click on the **underlined text** for any additional help topics. The help file will appear in the window.

5. Click on the **Close button** when you are finished reading the help files. The Quicken Help window will close.

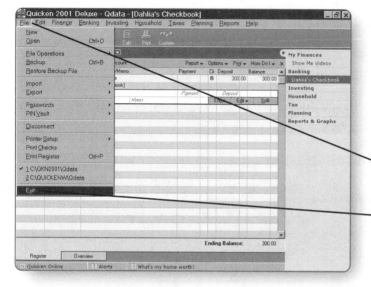

Closing Quicken

When you've finished with Quicken, exit the program. This automatically saves the data.

1. Click on **File**. The File menu will appear.

2. Click on **Exit**. The Quicken program will close and you will return to your desktop.

2

Exploring the Quicken World

In the last chapter, you learned how to start and stop the Quicken program and where to find help if you get stuck while working with the program. Now it's time to take a quick cruise around Quicken and learn just how much control Quicken gives you over your financial status. You may think that Quicken is just a checkbook manager. Well, it's much, much more. In addition to keeping your checkbook balanced, you can keep track of your investment accounts, keep your spending within budgeted limits, and plan for major purchases and future needs. In this chapter, you'll learn how to:

- Navigate the Quicken Centers
- Use Quicken to connect to the Internet and find financial help
- Set up a printer to print financial reports

Visiting the Quicken Centers

Quicken is divided into a number of centers that help you manage different aspects of your financial portfolio. These centers help you track banking and investment accounts, plan for major purchases such as a home or car, and create savings goals to help you finance a college education or retirement. You can quickly move from center to center using QuickTabs. QuickTabs are found along the right side of the Quicken program window.

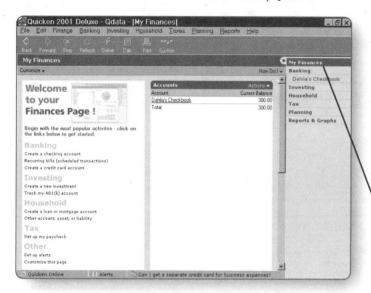

1. Click on the **My Finances QuickTab**. The My Finances page will be displayed. This page is the introduction to the other centers that are listed in the QuickTabs.

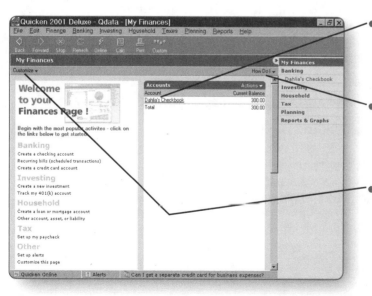

• Click on the blue underlined text to go to a page that contains more information about that topic.

• To learn more about the information in the Quicken Center, click on the How Do I button.

• To change the look of the Quicken Center, click on the Customize button.

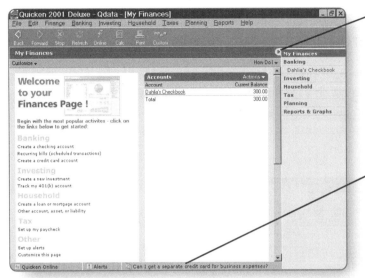

2. **Click** on the **arrow** at the top left of the QuickTabs bar. The QuickTabs will disappear and provide more working room within the program window.

TIP

Quicken provides quick tips to help you manage your finances and work efficiently with the program. Click on the item at the bottom of the window to learn more about the suggested topic.

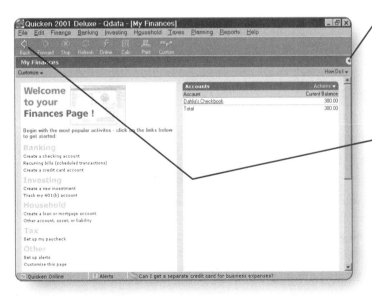

3. **Click** on the **QuickTab arrow**. The QuickTabs will reappear.

NOTE

Click on the Back button to see previously viewed pages.

Accessing Bank and Credit Card Accounts

The Banking Center is your overview to the checking, savings, and credit card accounts that you've set up in Quicken. You can use this center to access your checkbook register, create new accounts, and schedule payments so that your bills get paid on time.

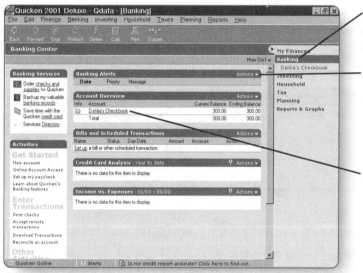

1. Click on the **Banking QuickTab**. The Banking Center will appear.

- Click on an Actions down arrow. A menu will appear that lists the actions that can be performed for each section in the center.

- Click on the underlined text in the Account Overview section to display the register for any accounts you have set up.

NOTE

You'll learn how to set up additional bank accounts in Chapter 3, "Setting Up Accounts and Files." You'll also learn how to schedule bill payments and other reminders in Chapter 8, "Scheduling Payments."

Tracking Home and Car Expenses

The Household Center provides an overview of any loans for which you need to make regular payments, assets that you have acquired, and automobile expenses you have incurred. You can also use the links in this center to help you decide whether you can afford to buy a new car or home, and to find a reasonable deal on the insurance you need to guard against the loss of these assets in case of a disaster.

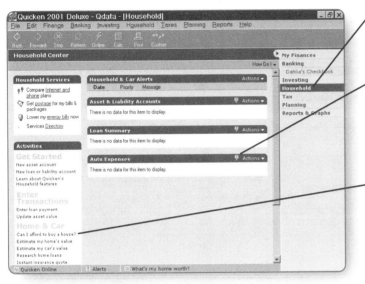

1. Click on the **Household QuickTab**. The Household Center will appear.

● Click on the lightbulb icon. A screen tip will appear that advises you on what you can do to efficiently track financial information.

● Click on the blue text in the Activities section. These activities walk you through the steps necessary to perform the selected task.

NOTE

You'll learn how to set up a mortgage loan and record mortgage payments in Chapter 11, "Creating Mortgage Accounts." You'll learn how to plan for car and home purchases in Chapter 21, "Buying a Car," and Chapter 22, "Owning a Home."

Paying Uncle Sam

The Tax Center lets you know when tax payments need to be paid to the IRS, and helps you keep track of your tax liability. You can also use the activities listed on this page to find tax deductions and reduce the amount of taxes that you pay.

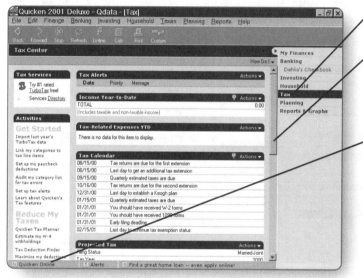

1. Click on the **Tax QuickTab**. The Tax Center will appear.

● Click and drag the scroll bar. You'll see more information and activities for the center you are viewing.

● Click on Quicken Online at the bottom of the page. This will give you access to Quicken's online features, such as online banking and bill paying.

NOTE

You'll learn how to set up Quicken to keep track of taxable items and tax deductions and to forecast your tax liability in Chapter 12, "Dealing with Taxes."

Planning Major Purchases

Putting money aside to pay for major purchases or for college is not an easy task. It is even harder to think about how much money you will need to support yourself during your retirement years. There are so many decisions to make and variables to consider. The Planning Center can help you make decisions that will have a major impact on your future.

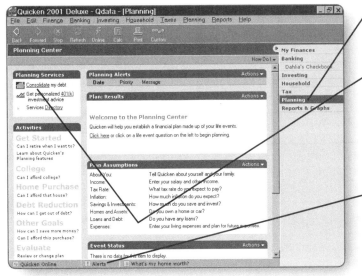

1. Click on the **Planning QuickTab**. The Planning Center will appear.

● Click on the blue text in the Planning Services section. You'll find professional help on the Internet to help you make these important decisions.

● Click on Alerts at the bottom of the page. You'll be taken to the Quicken Alerts page, where you can set up notifications that will tell you when there have been changes in your financial situation.

NOTE

You'll learn how to reduce your debt and plan your future in Chapter 18, "Creating a Savings Plan," Chapter 20, "Going to College," and Chapter 23, "Planning for Retirement."

Investing in the Future

In order to achieve your financial goals, you will need to invest your money wisely to gain the maximum return on your savings. The Investing Center helps you stay on top of any investments you may have made in the stock market.

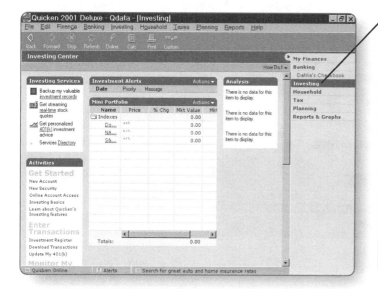

1. Click on the **Investing QuickTab**. The Investing Center will appear.

NOTE

You'll learn how the stock market works and how you can track prices on stocks you may have purchased or are considering purchasing in Chapter 19, "Investing in the Stock Market."

Viewing Your Financial Picture

Quicken provides a plethora of reports that give you a snapshot of your financial situation. These reports can tell you how much you are worth, how much money you spend on specified items, how well your investments are performing, and your tax liability. Each report can be customized to fit your needs.

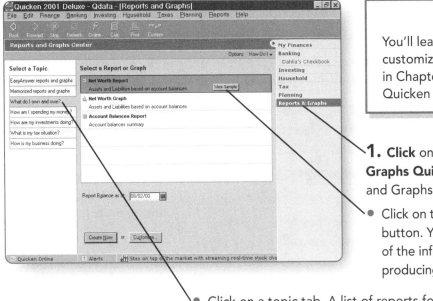

NOTE

You'll learn how to customize these reports in Chapter 13, "Using the Quicken Tools."

1. Click on the **Reports & Graphs QuickTab**. The Reports and Graphs Center will appear.

• Click on the View Sample button. You'll see an example of the information found by producing the selected report.

• Click on a topic tab. A list of reports for that topic will appear.

Going Online with Quicken

You can use the Internet to help track and manage your personal finances. Quicken comes equipped to use the Internet for these tasks, but it first needs to recognize your dial-up connection to your Internet Service Provider (ISP).

NOTE

You can use either Dial-Up Networking or the Internet Connection wizard to create a dial-up connection on your computer. If you are using Windows 98, you'll find both in the Communications submenu under Accessories, in the Start Programs menu. If you are using Windows 95, you'll find Dial-Up Networking in the Accessories submenu and the Internet Connection wizard in the Internet Explorer submenu.

Setting Up an Internet Connection

Before you can use Quicken on the Internet, your account needs to be set up with an ISP. The ISP will provide the information you need to create a dial-up connection between your computer's modem and the ISP's servers. Once you have a working Internet connection, you're ready to set up Quicken to access the Internet.

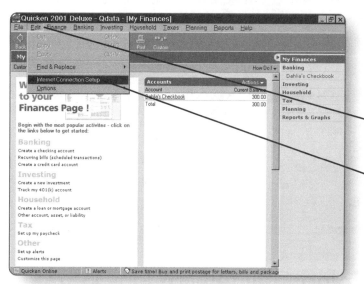

1. Click on **Edit**. The Edit menu will appear.

2. Click on **Internet Connection Setup**. The Intuit Internet Connection Profile Manager dialog box will open.

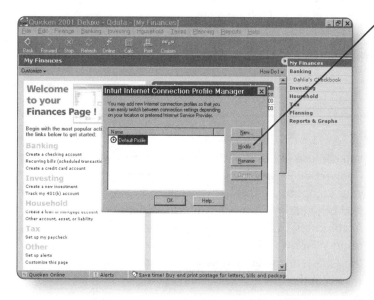

3. Click on the **Modify button**. The Internet Connection Setup wizard will start and the Are you connected to the Internet? screen will be displayed.

4a. Click on the **I have an existing dial-up Internet connection option button** if you connect to the Internet through an ISP. The option will be selected.

OR

4b. Click on the **I have a direct Internet connection option button** if you have cable or network access to the Internet. The option will be selected.

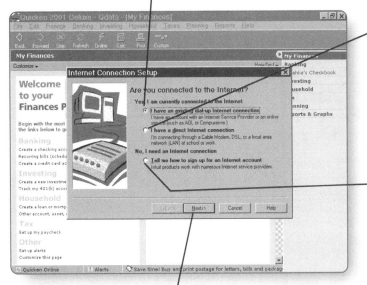

TIP

Quicken can help you find an ISP. Click on the Tell me how to sign up for an Internet account option button.

5. Click on **Next**. The Which dial-up Internet connection do you want to use? screen will appear. You can use this screen to select a dial-up connection that is already created on your computer.

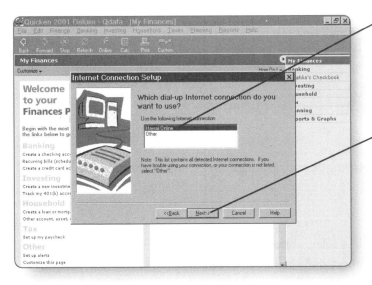

6. Click on the **Internet connection** that you want to use to access the Internet with Quicken. The connection will be selected.

7. Click on **Next**. The Browser Preference screen will appear.

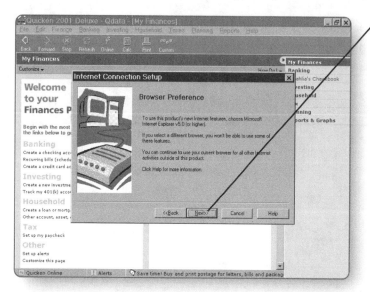

8. Click on **Next**. Quicken will search the programs on your computer and display a list of Web browsers that are installed on your computer.

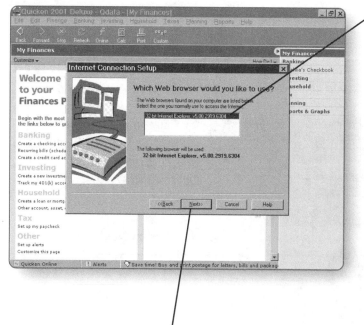

9. Click on the **browser** you want to use when accessing the Internet. The browser will be selected.

NOTE

You can install the 128-bit version of Microsoft Internet Explorer when you install Quicken. It is suggested that you use this browser if you'll be using the Internet for online banking and bill paying.

10. Click on **Next**. The Summary of your Internet Connection Setup screen will appear.

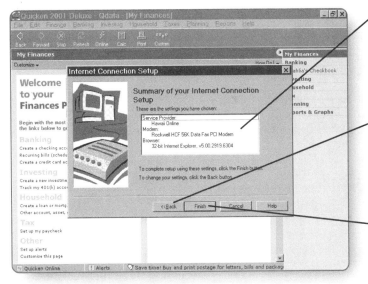

11. Verify that the **information** you supplied is correct.

NOTE

If you notice any errors, click on the Back button and make changes to the appropriate screens.

12. Click on **Finish**. The Intuit Internet Connection Profile Manager dialog box will return.

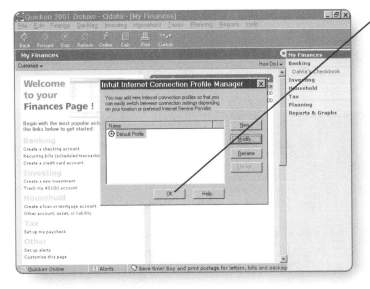

13. Click on **OK**. The Customize Quicken Download dialog box will open.

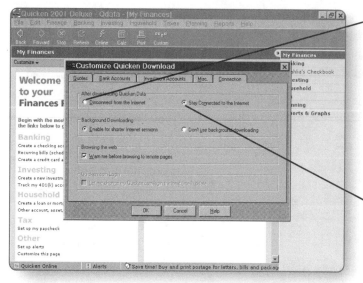

14a. Click on the **Disconnect from the Internet option button** if you want to close your Internet connection after Quicken has finished downloading data to your computer. The option will be selected.

OR

14b. Click on the **Stay Connected to the Internet option button** if you want to keep your Internet connection open after Quicken is finished accessing the Internet. The option will be selected.

NOTE

The Quicken Download Agent automatically downloads any information you requested from the Internet whenever you have an open Internet connection.

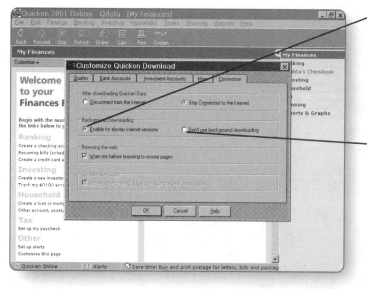

15a. Click on the **Enable for shorter Internet sessions option button** if you want to activate the Quicken Download Agent. The option will be selected.

OR

15b. Click on the **Don't use background downloading option button** if you want Quicken to download information only when you request it. The option will be selected.

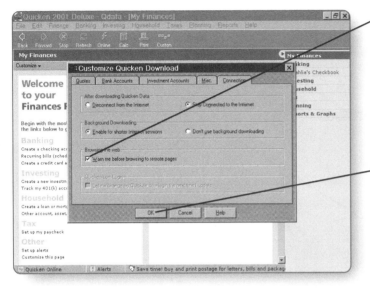

16. **Click** in the **Warn me before browsing to remote pages check box** if you do not want to see a warning dialog box whenever you move from Web site to Web site. The check box will be cleared.

17. **Click** on **OK**. Quicken will be set up so that it can access the Internet using your existing dial-up connection.

Finding Financial Help on the Internet

Now that Quicken is set up to use your Internet connection, it's easy to get online. Any time you click on an item in Quicken that needs information from the Internet, Quicken will automatically dial your ISP. Here's a quick example of how this works.

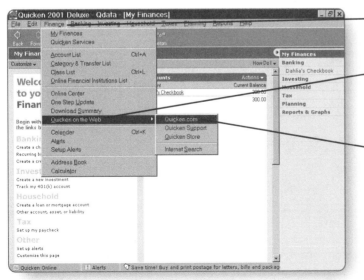

1. **Click** on **Finance**. The Finance menu will appear.

2. **Move** the **mouse pointer** to Quicken on the Web. A second menu will appear.

3. **Click** on **Quicken.com**. A confirmation dialog box will open.

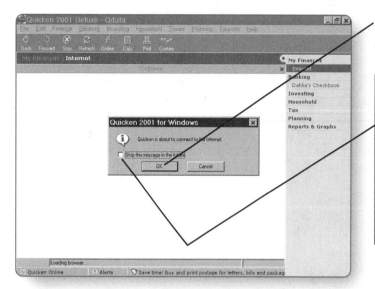

4. Click on **OK**. The Connecting dialog box will open.

TIP

If you don't want to be warned each time that Quicken connects to the Internet, click in the Skip this message in the future check box to select the option.

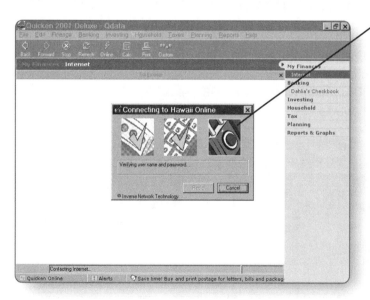

5. Wait while your **computer** connects to your ISP. When it connects, the browser will be loaded inside the Quicken window and the Quicken.com Web site will appear in the browser. The Quicken.com Web site contains a wealth of information that can help you manage your finances.

6. Click on a **hyperlink**. The linked page will appear in the browser window.

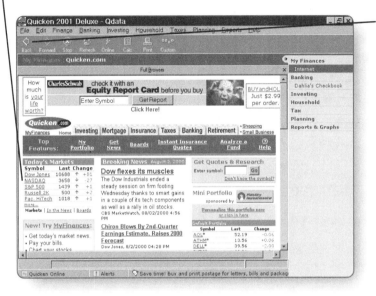

7. Click on the **Back button**. The previous Web page that you visited will appear in the browser window.

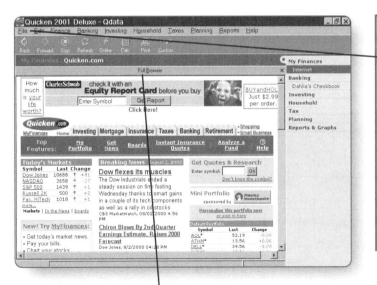

TIP

When you are finished surfing the Web for financial information, close the browser window. Then, to disconnect from your ISP using the Quicken program, click on File to display the File menu and select Disconnect from the menu.

8. Click on the **Full Browser button**. The Web page will no longer appear in the Quicken window, but in the default browser. You can then use browser features, such as bookmarks or favorites, while surfing the Quicken Web pages.

Setting Up a Printer

Before you begin creating reports, take some time to set up your printer so that printed reports have the look that you like.

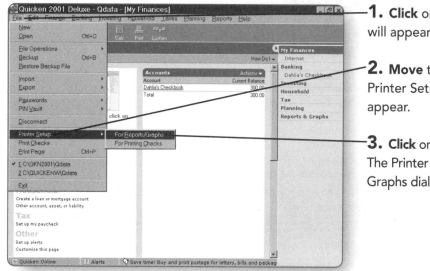

1. Click on **File**. The File menu will appear.

2. Move the **mouse pointer** to Printer Setup. A submenu will appear.

3. Click on **For Reports/Graphs**. The Printer Setup for Reports and Graphs dialog box will open.

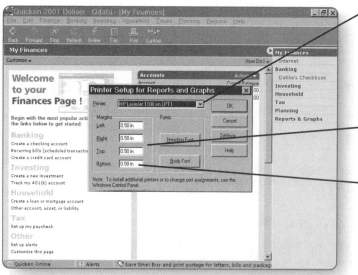

4. Click on the **Printer down arrow** and **click** on the **printer** that you want to use. The printer name will appear in the list box.

5. Click in each of the **Margins text boxes**.

6. Type the **margin space** that you want to appear between the report edges and the paper edges.

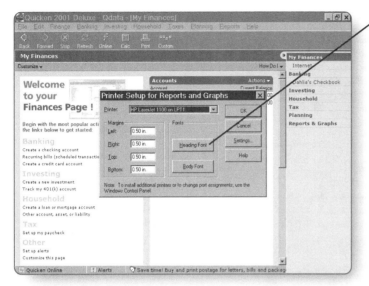

7. Click on the **Heading Font button and/or the Body Font button** if you want to change the font style used to print the report. The Select Heading Font or the Select Body Font dialog box will open. These two dialog boxes look identical and work in the same manner.

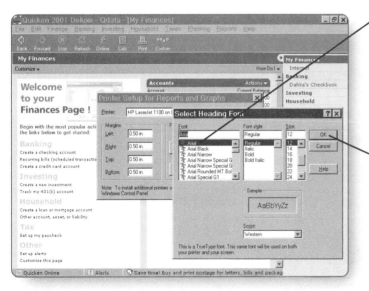

8. Click in the **list boxes**, in turn, for Font, Font style, and Size and **click** on a **font, font style, or size** in the drop-down listings. Your choices will be selected for each list box.

9. Click on **OK**. You will return to the Printer Setup for Reports and Graphs dialog box.

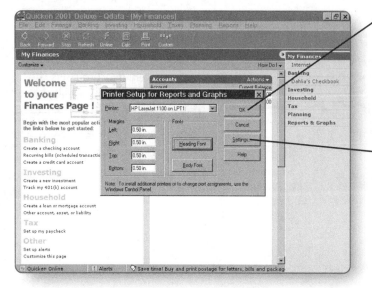

10. **Click** on **OK**. Quicken will now be ready to work with your printer to produce your year-end reports.

TIP

If you want to change printer options, such as print resolution or paper orientation, click on the Settings button.

3

Setting Up Accounts and Files

In the first chapter, you set up your first bank account in the default Quicken data file. If you have other bank accounts, such as savings or money market accounts, you can also set those up in the same Quicken file. Then, as you progress and begin entering transactions for these accounts, this information will also be added to the default Quicken data file. But, what if you want to keep separate financial records for another member of your family or for a small business that you run out of a spare bedroom? It's easy to set up another file in which to store a separate set of financial information. In this chapter, you'll learn how to:

- Set up additional accounts you may have at your bank
- Make changes to the accounts you have set up
- Create separate Quicken data files for other sources of financial data
- Copy and rename Quicken data files

Working with Banking Accounts

You may have more bank accounts than the one you set up during the New User Setup. If you have additional checking and savings accounts, you can add these to Quicken and keep track of these account balances. You can also set up accounts for any investments that you might have. After you've been working with Quicken for a while, you might need to make changes to these accounts. Perhaps the bank information has changed, or maybe you're not using that account any longer.

Creating a New Account

You can keep track of many different types of accounts. If you set up your checking account in the New User Setup, you might want to add savings or credit card accounts. If you want to keep track of cash purchases, create a cash account. Setting up an account is similar for each type of account. Just follow the EasyStep instructions.

1. **Click** on **Banking**. The Banking menu will appear.

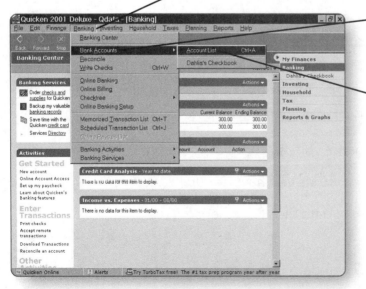

2. **Move** the **mouse pointer** to Bank Accounts. A second menu will appear.

3. **Click** on **Account List**. The Account List window will appear.

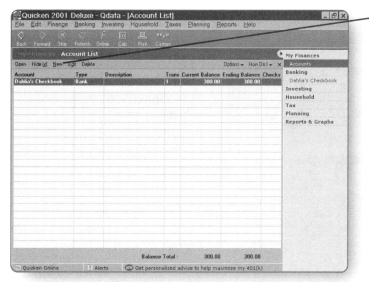

4. Click on **New**. The Create New Account wizard will open and display the Choose the type of account to create screen.

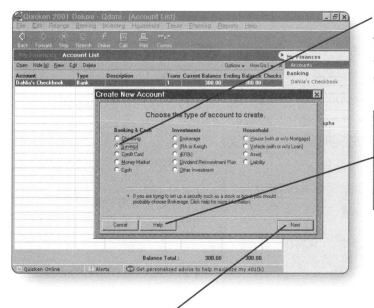

5. Click on the **option button** that corresponds to the type of account you want to create. The option will be selected.

TIP
If you need help with a screen, click on the Help button.

6. Click on **Next**. The EasyStep setup for the account type will start and will display the Enter a name and optional description for this account screen.

7. Type a descriptive **name** for the account in the Account Name text box.

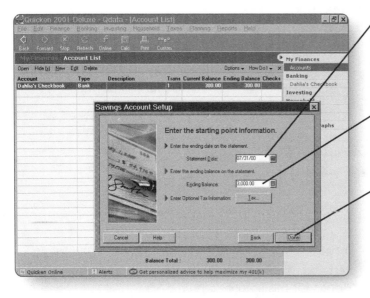

8. Click on the **Financial Institution down arrow** and **select** your **bank** from the list. If your bank is not listed, you can type the name of your bank in the text box.

9. Type the **purpose** of the account in the Description (optional) text box.

10. Click on **Next**. The Enter the starting point information screen will appear.

11. Type the **ending date** of the statement you will use as a starting point in the Statement Date text box.

12. Type the **ending bank balance** found on the statement in the Ending Balance text box.

13. Click on **Done**. The setup will be completed.

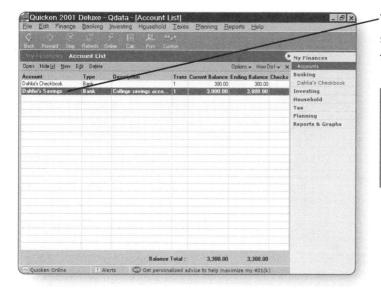

The Account List window will show the new account added to the list.

TIP

You can have as many as 512 accounts set up for each Quicken file.

Updating Account Information

You can add some additional information to an account. For example, you might want to add a contact name and phone number for your bank or record interest rates. Before you can make any changes to an account, you'll need to display the Account List.

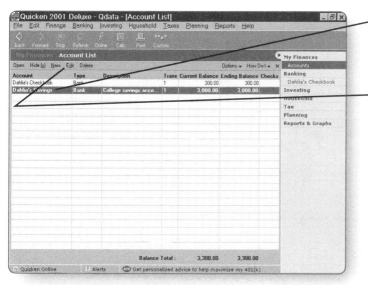

1. Click on the **account** that you want to update. The account will be selected.

2. Click on the **Edit button**. The Banking window for the account will appear.

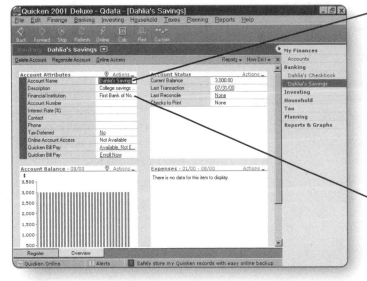

3. **Click** in the **Account Name field** located in the Account Attributes section of the window. The text in the field will be selected.

4. **Type** a **different name** for the account in the Account Name field.

5. **Click** in any other **Account Attributes field** to complete or change information. The field will be highlighted.

6. Enter the **information** about your account and/or the financial institution.

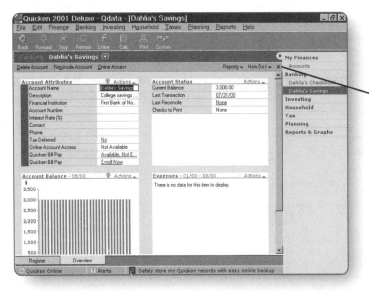

7. Repeat steps 5 and 6 until you complete any or all fields to your satisfaction.

8. Click on the **Close button** when you are finished updating the account. The Banking window will close and you will return to the Account List window.

Hiding Accounts

If you're not using an account, you can make it disappear from the list. This is not the same as deleting it. Your data will still be retained by Quicken. You still have access to the account and can view it on the list, even after the account has been hidden.

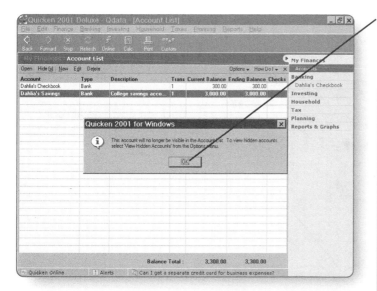

1. Click on the **account** that you want to hide from the account list. The account will be selected.

2. Click on the **Hide (x) button**. A confirmation dialog box will open.

3. Click on **OK**. You'll no longer see the account in the Account List.

NOTE

If you want to see the account, click on the Options button and select View Hidden Accounts from the menu that appears. A hand icon to the right of the account name will indicate the hidden account. If you want to unhide the account, click on the Hide (x) button.

Deleting Accounts

When you delete an account, you also delete all the transactions that have been recorded in the account. There will be no trace of the account in the Quicken data file.

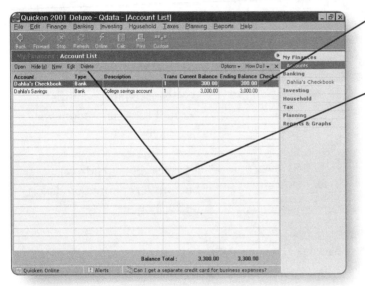

1. Click on the **account** that you want to delete. The account will be selected.

2. Click on the **Delete button**. A confirmation dialog box will open.

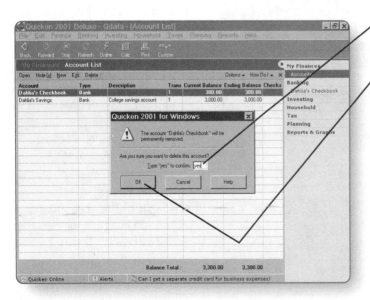

3. Type the word **yes** in the Type "yes" to confirm text box.

4. Click on **OK**. The account will be removed from the Account List.

Creating a New Quicken File

Quicken stores every check you write, every paycheck you deposit, and every investment you make in a single data file. The file that is initially created by Quicken is called Qdata.QDF and is stored in the Quickenw directory. You can perform a number of tasks with this file, such as copying, renaming, and moving. Quicken also allows you to work with several data files. For example, you can have a separate file for your personal needs, a file for the kids to keep track of their allowance and spending, and perhaps a bookkeeping file for any organization to which you belong.

Opening the New File

You should keep separate records for the different activities in your life. You may want to keep your personal finances, a small business venture, and records for a club or charity in separate files.

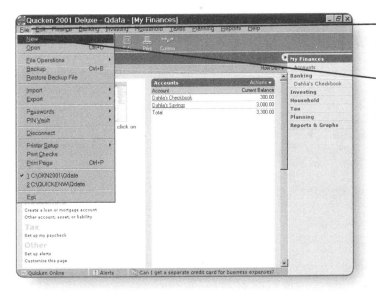

1. Click on **File**. The File menu will appear.

2. Click on **New**. The Creating new file: Are you sure? dialog box will open.

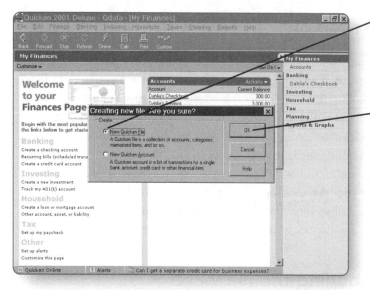

3. **Click** on the **New Quicken File option button**, if it is not already selected. The option will be selected.

4. **Click** on **OK**. The Create Quicken File dialog box will open.

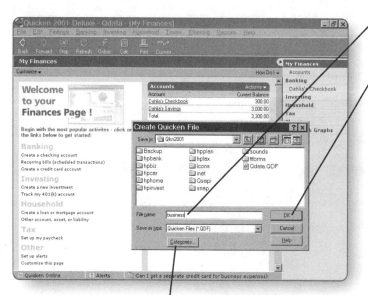

5. **Type** a **name** for the new file in the File name text box.

6. **Click** on **OK**. The new account will be created and the Create New Account wizard will appear so that you can set up your first account in the new file.

TIP

If you want to include categories other than the standard ones, click on the Categories button. You'll learn more about categories in Chapter 4, "Creating a Chart of Accounts."

Switching between Multiple Files

After you create several different Quicken files, you can work with each of them, but only one at a time. Here's how to switch between the different Quicken data files that you may have created.

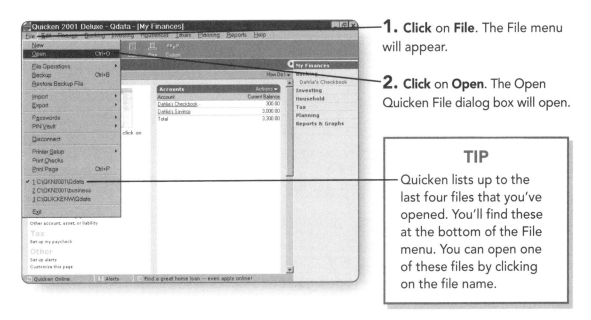

1. Click on **File**. The File menu will appear.

2. Click on **Open**. The Open Quicken File dialog box will open.

TIP

Quicken lists up to the last four files that you've opened. You'll find these at the bottom of the File menu. You can open one of these files by clicking on the file name.

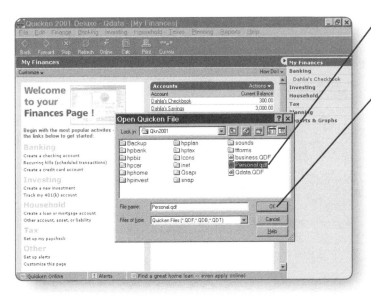

3. Click on the **file** with which you want to work. The file will be selected.

4. Click on **OK**. The data file will appear in the Quicken window.

Making Copies of Files

If you need a quick start when creating a separate set of records, make a copy of a Quicken data file. This enables you to use certain types of records (such as memorized and scheduled transactions or a customized category list) to start a new data file.

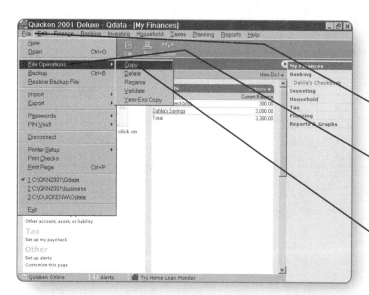

1. Open the **file** you want to copy. The file will appear in the Quicken window.

2. Click on **File**. The File menu will appear.

3. Move the **mouse pointer** to File Operations. A second menu will appear.

4. Click on **Copy**. The Copy File dialog box will open.

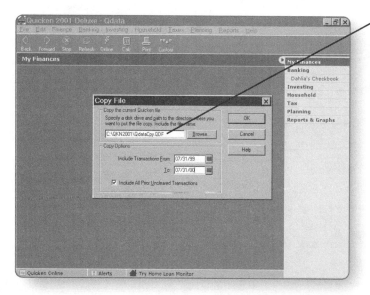

5. Type a **name** for the copy of the file in the Name text box. Be sure to include the directory path in the file name.

TIP

You can also click on the Browse button to display a file manager dialog box. From this dialog box you can search your computer for the file for which you are looking.

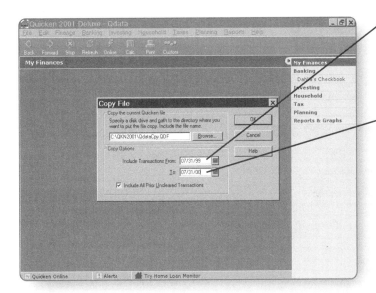

6. Type the **beginning date** of the group of transactions that you want to copy in the Include Transactions From text box.

7. Type the **ending date** of the group of transactions that you want to copy in the To text box.

8. Click on **OK**. The File Copied Successfully dialog box will open.

9a. Click on the **Original file option button** if you want to work with the original file. The option will be selected.

OR

9b. Click on the **New copy option button** if you want to work with the file you just created. The option will be selected.

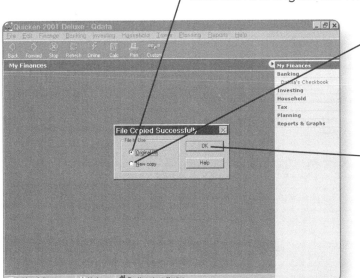

10. Click on **OK**. The file you selected will appear in the Quicken window so that you can work with it.

Renaming Files

You can also give Quicken data files different file names. Once you begin adding files, you may find that you need to give older files more descriptive names.

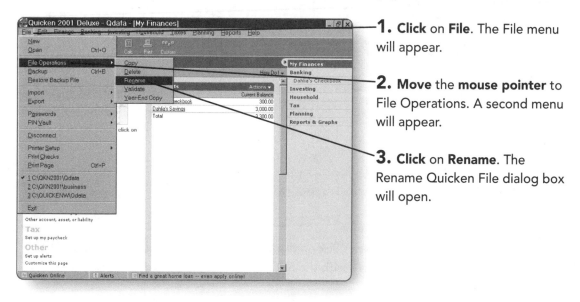

1. Click on **File**. The File menu will appear.

2. Move the **mouse pointer** to File Operations. A second menu will appear.

3. Click on **Rename**. The Rename Quicken File dialog box will open.

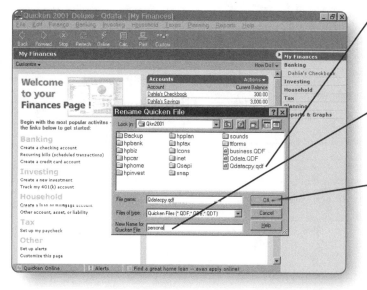

4. Click on the **file** that you want to rename. The file will appear in the File name text box.

5. Type a different **name** for the file in the New Name for Quicken File text box.

6. Click on **OK**. The file will be renamed.

4

Creating a Chart of Accounts

In order to keep track of expenditures for different items (such as groceries, clothing, and gasoline), you'll need a well-constructed chart of accounts. The chart of accounts lists sources of income and items of expenditure, which you can use to determine whether you're saving money or falling into debt. Quicken provides a starting chart of accounts in the Category & Transfer List. You'll find it easy to customize this list to fit your lifestyle. In this chapter, you'll learn how to:

- Add and delete categories from the Category & Transfer List
- Divide categories into subcategories
- Use classes to track particular expenses

Organizing Categories

It is very important to keep track of expenditures if you want to keep track of where you spend your money and if you need to stay on a budget. To do this, a chart of accounts, in the form of the Category & Transfer List, will contain items to which you'll assign each purchase and deposit you make for each bank account that you've set up in Quicken. By assigning each transaction to a category, it is easy to keep track of income deposits from a hobby or how much is spent on weekend entertainment.

Adding Categories to the Chart of Accounts

The Category & Transfer List contains a fairly complete list of categories to fit most of your needs. But, there might be an item that you want to track that isn't included in the list. You can modify the list to reflect your income sources and spending habits.

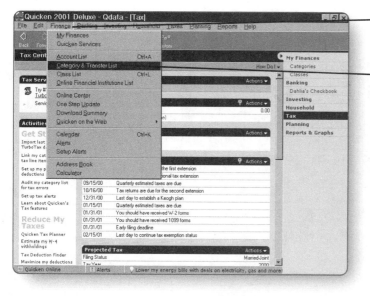

1. Click on **Finance**. The Finance menu will appear.

2. Click on **Category & Transfer List**. The Category & Transfer List window will appear.

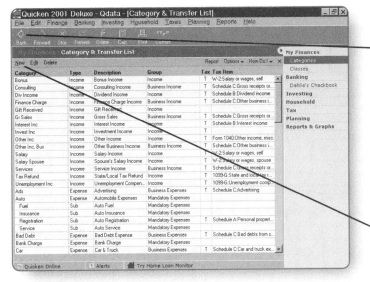

TIP

The buttons on the toolbar can be quickly rearranged if you don't like the order in which they appear. Click and drag the button to the desired location on the toolbar.

3. Click on **New**. The Set Up Category dialog box will open.

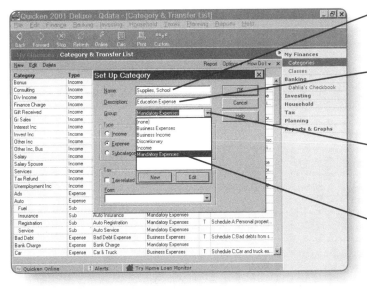

4. Type a **name** for the new category in the Name text box.

5. Type a brief **description** for the category in the Description text box.

6. Click on the **Group down arrow**. A list of income and expense types will appear.

7. Click on the **group** to which you want to assign the category. The group will appear in the list box.

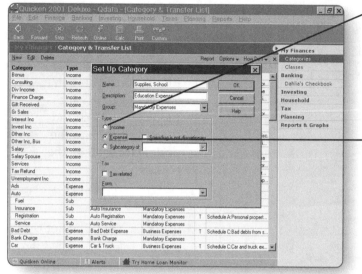

8a. **Click** on the **Income option button** if the category will be used to record money you receive. The option will be selected.

OR

8b. **Click** on the **Expense option button** if the category will be used to record money you spend. The option will be selected.

9. **Click** on OK. The category will be added to the Category & Transfer List.

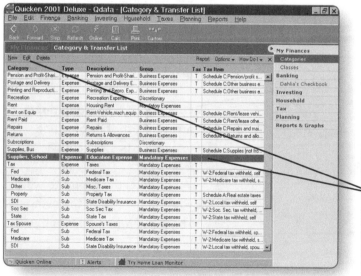

The new category will be listed by income and expense, in alphabetical order, in the Category & Transfer List. All the category information you entered into the dialog box will also be displayed.

TIP

You can make changes to a category. Just select the category and click on the Edit button. Make your changes in the Edit Category dialog box.

Setting Up Subcategories

After you've worked with Quicken for a while, you may find that too many transactions are going to a certain category. These transactions may all be related (such as utility bills), but could be broken into subcategories (such as phone, natural gas, and electricity bills). You'll notice that subcategories are indented below the related category in the Category & Transfer List.

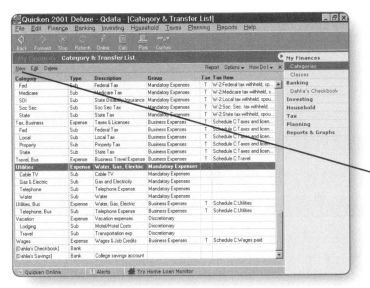

1. Open the **Category & Transfer List**.

2. Click on **New**. The Set Up Category dialog box will open.

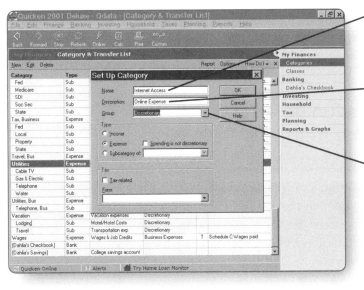

3. Type a **name** for the subcategory in the Name text box.

4. Type a **description** of the subcategory in the Description text box.

5. Click on the **Group down arrow** and **choose** a **group**. The group will be selected.

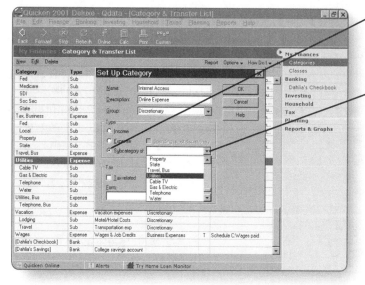

6. Click on the **Subcategory of option button**. The option will be selected.

7. Click on the **Subcategory of down arrow** and **click** on the **category** where the subcategory should be located. The category will be selected.

8. Click on **OK**. The subcategory will be added to the list under the selected category.

TIP

You might want to keep a printed copy of your chart of accounts. Click on the Print icon. Click on the Preview button to see what the list will look like on the printed page. You can change the font style and size by using the Heading Font and Body Font buttons. You can also save the chart of accounts as a file that you can import into a word-processing program and make any changes there.

Assigning a Tax Form Line Item to a Category

A number of categories are already set up so that amounts recorded in the category are assigned to a tax form and to a line item on that tax form. If you have added new categories, or if a category is not assigned to a tax form, you can easily tell Quicken which tax form to use for a category. You can also obtain help to decide on an appropriate tax form.

1. Open the **Category & Transfer List**.

2. Click on the **category** you want to track for tax purposes. The category will be selected.

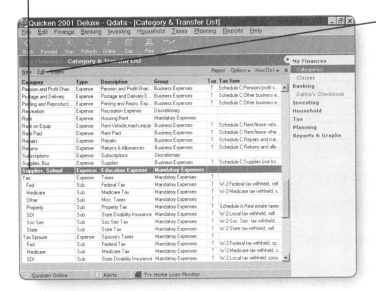

3. Click on **Edit**. The Edit Category dialog box will open.

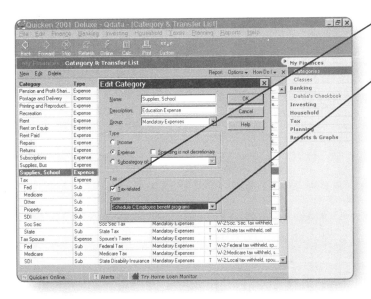

4. Place a **check mark** in the Tax-related check box.

5. Click on the **Form down arrow** and **select** the **tax form line item** that you want to apply to the category. The tax form and line item will be selected.

6. Click on **OK**. The tax form changes will be applied to the category item.

Deleting Categories

If you don't want to clutter the Category & Transfer List with categories that you'll never use, you can delete any unneeded categories.

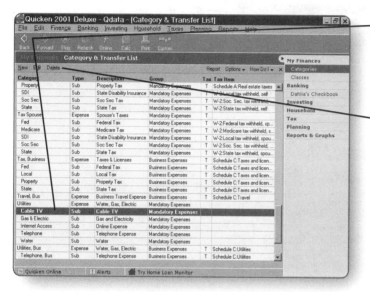

1. Click on the **category** that you want to remove from the Category & Transfer List. The category will be selected.

2. Click on **Delete**. A confirmation dialog box will open.

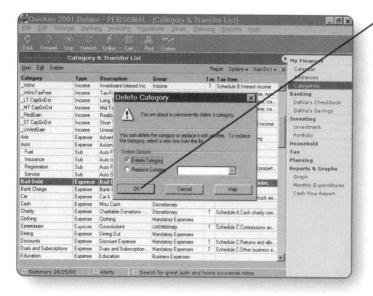

3. Click on **OK**. The category will be removed from the Category & Transfer List.

Restoring the Original Category List

Even if you add and delete categories, Quicken still retains the original category items. If you find that you have a need for a deleted category, you can restore that category. Depending on how you answered questions during the New User Setup, some categories may not appear in your list but you can still access them. You'll find them in Quicken's memory bank.

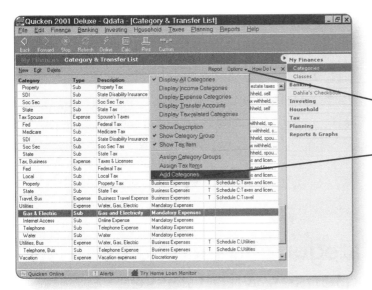

1. Click on **Options**. The Options menu will appear.

2. Click on **Add Categories**. The Add Categories dialog box will open.

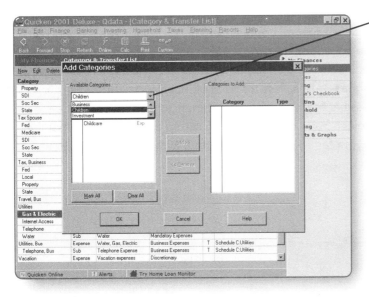

3. Click on the **Available Categories down arrow** and **click** on the **category type** for which you want to add a category. The classification will appear in the list box.

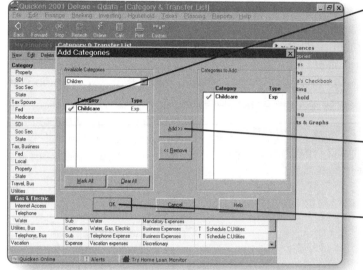

4. **Click** on the **category** that you want to add to the Category & Transfer List. The category will be selected and a check mark will appear to the left of the category.

5. **Click** on **Add**. The Category will appear in the Categories to Add list box.

6. **Click** on **OK**. The categories you added will appear in the Category & Transfer List and will be available to you when you begin recording transactions.

Categorizing Income and Expenses with Classes

Classes are an easy way to keep track of people, activities, or events that might incur expenses over several categories. If you have several hobbies, you might want to know how much you spend for gasoline, equipment rental, and meals for each hobby. Set up a separate class for each hobby. A business might set up a class for each of its projects. This makes it possible to determine what expenses are incurred for each project. You may also want to set up a class for each member of your family to keep track of individual expenses.

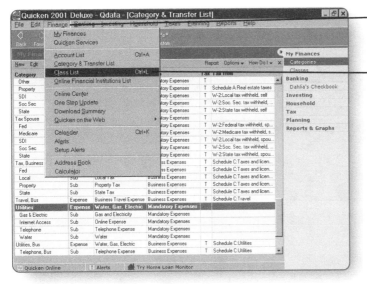

1. Click on **Finance**. The Finance menu will appear.

2. Click on **Class List**. The Class List window will appear.

3. Click on **New**. The Set Up Class dialog box will open.

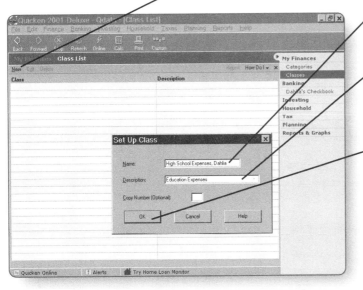

4. Type a **name** for the class in the Name text box.

5. Type a **description** of the class in the Description text box.

6. Click on **OK**. The new class will be added to the Class List.

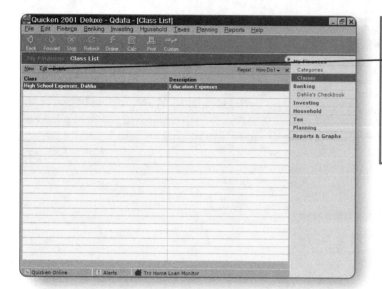

TIP

You can make changes to a class by using the Edit button, and you can remove classes by selecting the Delete button.

Part I Review Questions

1. What information will you need to collect before you start Quicken for the first time and set up your checking account? *See "Starting Quicken for the First Time" in Chapter 1*

2. Where can you go if you need specific help on the page, register, or center in Quicken in which you are working? *See "Getting More Help" in Chapter 1*

3. Which Quicken element makes it easy for you to move around the program and get started managing your finances? *See "Visiting the Quicken Centers" in Chapter 2*

4. How do you set up Quicken so that you can access financial information and help located on the Internet? *See "Going Online with Quicken" in Chapter 2*

5. How do you change the printer settings to customize the way reports and graphs look on the printed page? *See "Setting Up a Printer" in Chapter 2*

6. What types of accounts can you set up and track in Quicken? *See "Creating a New Account" in Chapter 3*

7. Which page in Quicken do you go to if you want to change the name you gave an account? *See "Updating Account Information" in Chapter 3*

8. How do you keep personal financial information separate from information you need to track for a small business? *See "Creating a New Quicken File" in Chapter 3*

9. What is the purpose of a chart of accounts? *See "Organizing Categories" in Chapter 4*

10. Is there a way to track categories for an individual person, customer, product sold, or project? *See "Categorizing Income and Expenses with Classes" in Chapter 4*

PART II

Keeping Your Finances Up-to-Date

5

Entering Account Transactions

In the first part of this book, you spent your time getting organized so that you could use Quicken to keep track of your finances. You learned program basics, how to go online, and where to find help. You then created bank accounts and customized a list of categories to keep track of your income and expenditures. Even though this chapter uses a checking account to show you how to record transactions, the process is the same in all registers. In this chapter, you'll learn how to:

- Enter checks and deposits into an account register
- Charge a transaction to several categories
- Search for and edit transactions
- View the check register and print reports

Recording Basic Transactions

Before you begin to enter payment and deposit transactions, gather up your checkbook and receipts and open a Quicken account register.

NOTE

There are several ways to open an account register. If you want to find a complete list of your accounts, go to the Account List and double-click on the account. If the account has a QuickTab, click on it to open the register. You'll also find accounts listed in the Banking, Bank Accounts menu.

Recording a Check Payment

Quicken keeps track of many things for you. For example, it can automatically type in the check number for the checks that you write. Of course, this only works if you write and record checks in numerical order.

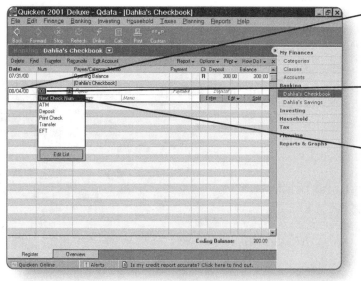

1. **Click** in the **Date field** and **type** the **date** that you wrote the check.

2. **Click** in the **Num field**. A drop-down list will appear.

3. **Click** on **Next Check Num**. The next unused check number in your checkbook will appear in the Num field.

NOTE

If this is the first check you are recording for this account, you will need to specify the beginning check number. Just replace the default check number in the Num field with your actual check number.

4. **Click** in the **Payee/Category/Memo field**. The insertion point will appear in the field.

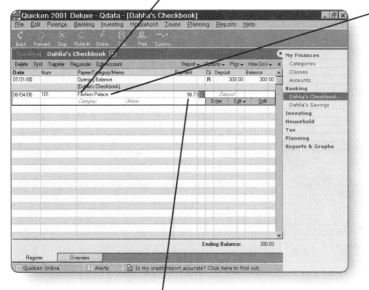

5. **Type** the **name** of the person or business to whom you wrote the check.

NOTE

Quicken stores these payee names. If you write a check to this person or business in the future, you can select the name from the Payee drop-down list.

6. **Click** in the **Payment field** and **type** the **amount** of the check.

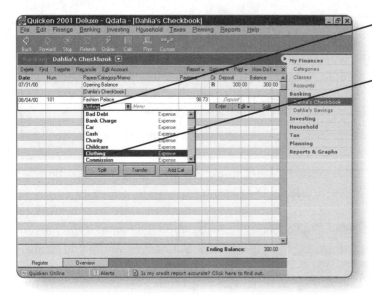

7. **Click** in the **Category field**. A drop-down list will appear.

8. **Click** on the **category** to which you want to assign the transaction. The category will be selected.

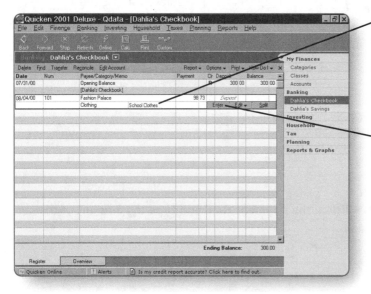

9. **Click** in the **Memo field** and **type** a **comment or note** that you want to use to add a description of the transaction. This step is optional.

10. **Click** on **Enter**. The transaction will be recorded in the register.

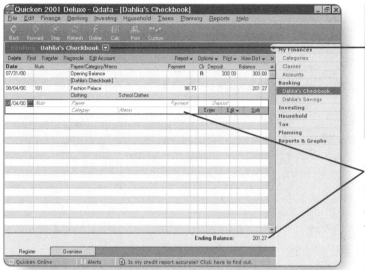

TIP
You can switch between accounts by clicking on the Banking down arrow located at the top of the register.

You'll notice that the balance of your account has been reduced. Also, the next transaction line in the register is selected and ready for you to record your next check.

Posting Deposits

Now let's do something a little more fun and put some money into your account.

1. **Click** in the **Date field** and **type** the **date** on which you made the deposit to the account.

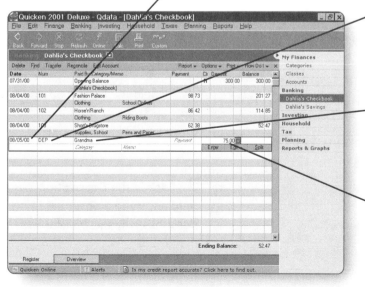

2. **Click** in the **Num field** and **click** on **Deposit** from the drop-down list. DEP will appear in the Num field.

3. **Click** in the **Payee field** and **type** the **name** of the person or business from whom you received the cash or check.

4. **Click** in the **Deposit field** and **type** the **amount** of the deposit.

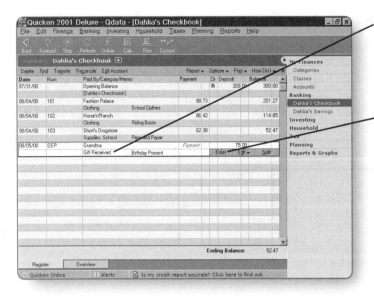

5. Click in the **Category field** and **select** an income **category** for the deposit. The category name will appear in the field.

6. Click on **Enter**. The deposit will be recorded in the register. You'll notice that the balance of the account has increased.

Transferring Funds between Accounts

When you move money from one account to another (for example, from checking to savings), you'll want to record this transaction as a transfer. This gives you a record of when the money was transferred and which accounts were involved.

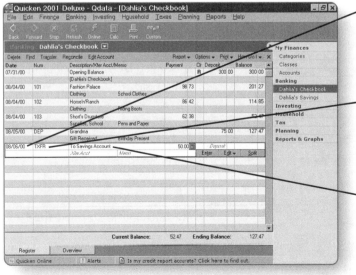

1. Click in the **Date field** and **type** the **date** on which you transferred money between accounts.

2. Click in the **Num field** and **click** on **Transfer** from the drop-down list. TXFR will appear in the Num field.

3. Click in the **Description field** and **type** a **note** that describes why the transfer was made.

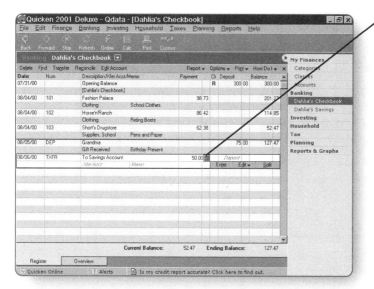

4. **Click** in the **Payment field** and **type** the **amount** of money you transferred between the accounts.

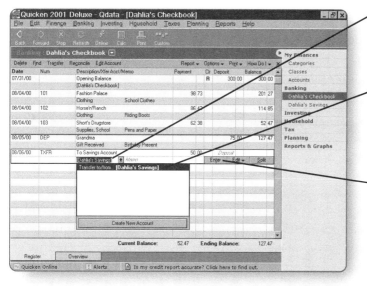

5. **Click** in the **Xfer account field**. A drop-down list will appear.

6. **Click** on the **account** to which the money is being transferred. The account will appear in the field.

7. **Click** on **Enter**. The transaction will be listed in the register. The balance of the selected account will be reduced by the amount of the transfer.

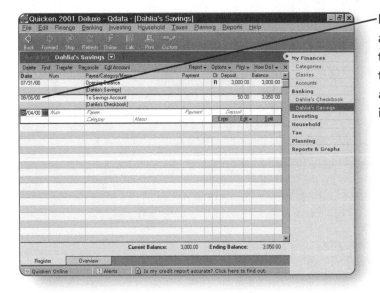

If you open the register for the account to which the money was transferred, you'll see the transaction entered in the account register and the increase in the account balance.

Splitting a Transaction between Categories

Entering a transaction and assigning it to a category is pretty simple. Most of the time when you go to the grocery store, you just buy groceries. But what if you also buy some stamps so you can send out a newsletter for your hobby or small business? You'll need to assign two categories to a single transaction. It takes a few more steps to enter a split transaction.

1. Click in the **Date field** and type the **transaction date**.

2. Click in the **Num field** and click on **ATM** from the list.

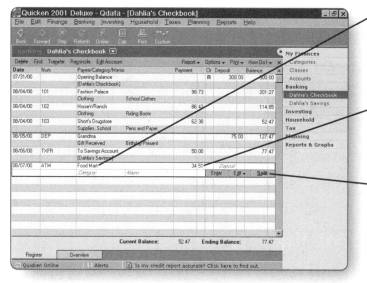

3. **Click** in the **Payee field** and **type** the **name** of the person or business to whom you wrote the check.

4. **Click** in the **Payment field** and **type** the total **amount** of the check.

5. **Click** on **Split**. The Split Transaction Window will appear.

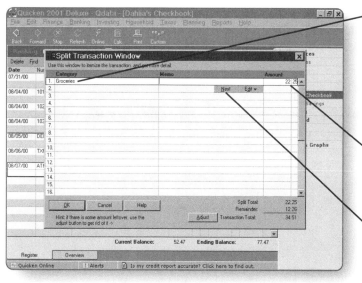

6. **Click** on the **Category down arrow** and **click** on the first **category** to which you want to assign part of the transaction. The category will appear in the list box.

7. **Click** in the **Amount field** and **type** the **amount** associated with that category.

8. **Click** on **Next**. The first category will be recorded and the next line will be selected.

The amount listed in the Amount field for the selected line is the amount of the check less all previous entries.

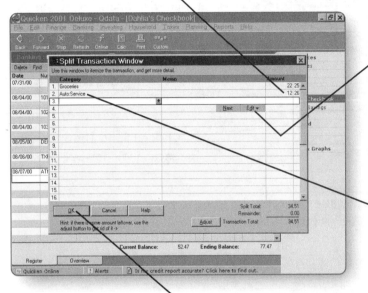

NOTE

If you add an entry in error, delete it. Select the entry, click on the Edit button, and select Delete from the menu that appears.

9. Repeat steps 6 through 8 until the total of the categories equals the total amount of the check.

10. Click on OK. The Split Transaction Window will close and the transaction will appear in the account register.

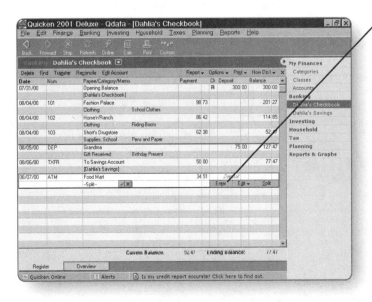

11. Click on Enter. The next line in the register will be ready for your next transaction.

Editing Transactions

After you have entered check and deposit transactions, take a minute to review the information. If you've misspelled any names, you can fix them. You should also make sure that transactions are assigned to the proper categories. If you find that you've written a check in error, you can void the transaction.

Changing Transaction Information

Making changes to any field in the account register is similar to working with text in a word-processing program. If you want to change text, just click and drag over it and make your changes.

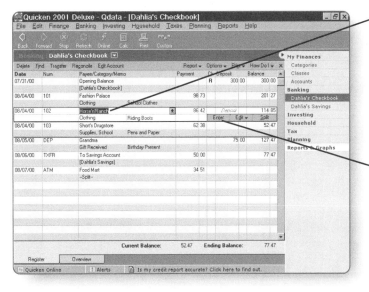

1. **Click** in the **field** in which you want to make the change. The field will be selected.

2. **Make** your **changes**. You can correct misspellings and amounts or change the assigned category.

3. **Click** on the **Enter button**. The changes will be applied to the transaction.

Voiding a Transaction

When you write a check in error, you'll want to keep a record of the destroyed check but not of the transaction. By voiding a check, any information stored about the transaction will be deleted.

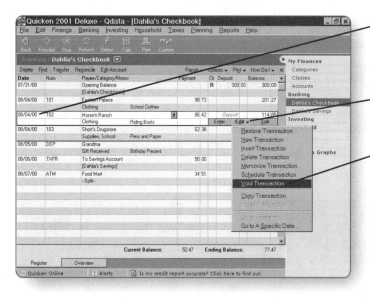

1. Click on the **transaction** that you want to void. The transaction will be selected.

2. Click on **Edit**. A menu will appear.

3. Click on **Void Transaction**. The word **VOID** will appear before the text in the Payee field and the amount field will be cleared.

NOTE

You can restore a voided transaction. Select Restore Transaction from the Edit menu.

NOTE

The c in the Clr field indicates that the transaction will not be recognized when the account is reconciled.

4. Click on **Enter**. The change will be saved and the register balance will be adjusted.

Searching for Transactions

After you have entered a few transactions in a register, you may need to go back and look at a particular transaction. If your register is long, it may take some time to browse through the list. Quicken can help you find a specific transaction.

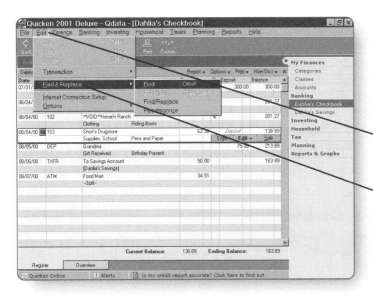

1. Open the account **register** that contains the transaction you want to find. The Banking window for the account will appear.

2. Click on **Edit**. The Edit menu will appear.

3. Move the **mouse pointer** to Find & Replace. A second menu will appear.

4. Click on **Find**. The Quicken Find dialog box will open.

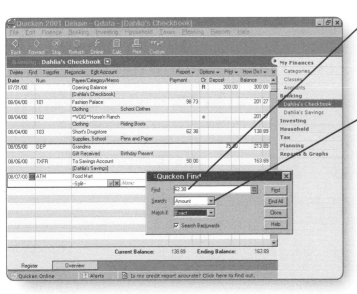

5. Click in the **Find text box** and **type** either **letters or numbers** that are contained in the transaction you want to find.

6. Click on the **Search down arrow** and **click** on the **field** in the register that you want to search. The search field will appear in the list box.

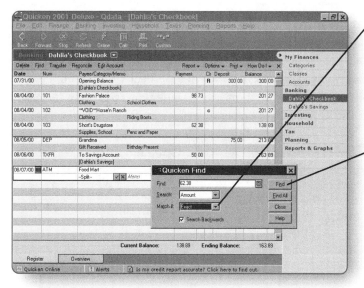

7. **Click** on the **Match if down arrow** and **click** on the **search parameters** that you want to add to the search. The search parameters will appear in the list box.

8. **Click** on **Find**. Quicken will look through the transactions in the register until it finds a match.

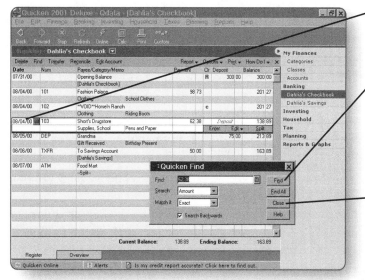

The first transaction that matches your search requirements will be selected in the register.

9. **Click** on **Find** if you want to search for another transaction that matches your search criteria. The match will be selected in the register.

10. **Click** on **Close** when you are finished searching for transactions in the register. The Quicken Find dialog box will close.

Printing a Register Report

It's easy to keep a printed copy of the check register.

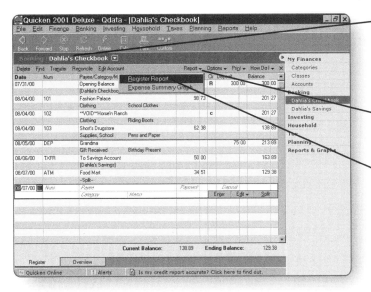

1. **Open** the **register** for which you want to print a Register Report. The account will appear in the Banking window.

2. **Click** on the **Report button**. A menu will appear.

3. **Click** on **Register Report**. The Register Report will be created.

The Register Report shows all the transactions that you've entered. At the bottom of the report, you'll see income and expenditures totals.

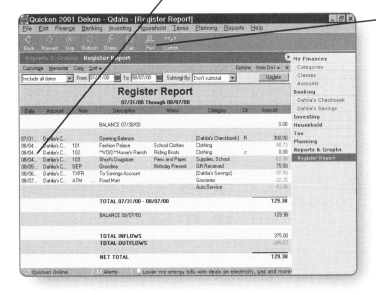

4. **Click** on the **Print button**. A paper copy of the report will be printed.

6

Automating Transactions

Most people have a set of bills that are paid on a regular monthly basis. Rent and mortgage payments are usually due at the first of each month. Telephone and other utility bills come due at different times during the month. Insurance payments may come due on a quarterly or an annual basis. Many times, these payments are for the same amounts, but sometimes the amount changes slightly. Quicken can help reduce the amount of time it takes to enter transactions that contain similar information. When you begin typing the name of the payee, Quicken attempts a match based on transactions you've entered recently. Quicken also contains a scheduling feature that reminds you when to pay your bills. Then, when you pay the bill, the transaction is recorded automatically. In this chapter, you'll learn how to:

- Use QuickFill to make entering transactions easier
- Change QuickFill options
- Work with memorized transactions

Using QuickFill to Enter Transactions

Quicken remembers every transaction you enter and can use that information for similar transactions. This works well for payments that you make regularly, such as rent, phone bills, and trips to the coffee shop.

Giving QuickFill a Spin

QuickFill allows you to recall a previously recorded transaction by typing a few letters in the Payee field. Before you begin, display the account register in which you want to work.

1. Click in the **Date field** and **type** the **date** of the transaction.

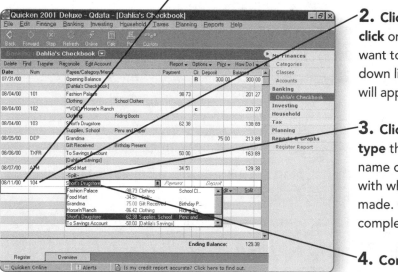

2. Click in the **Num field** and **click** on the **transaction type** you want to record from the drop-down list. The transaction type will appear in the Num field.

3. Click in the **Payee field** and **type** the **first letters** of the name of the person or business with whom the transaction was made. Quicken will attempt to complete the Payee field.

4. Continue typing until the correct name appears in the Payee field.

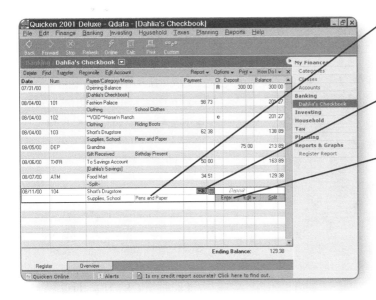

5. Press the **Tab key**. The rest of the transaction will be completed.

6. Make any necessary **changes**.

7. Click on the **Enter button**. The transaction will be recorded.

Changing QuickFill Options

If you're not entirely satisfied with how QuickFill performs, you can change a few options. By default, you move between fields in the register by pressing the Tab key, but you could use the Enter key instead. If you don't want to use the drop-down lists that appear when you click in a field, turn them off. Look at the different options and see how QuickFill can work differently for you.

1. Click on **Edit**. The Edit menu will appear.

2. Move the **mouse pointer** to Options. A submenu will appear.

3. Click on **Register**. The Register Options dialog box will open.

4. Click on the **QuickFill tab**. The QuickFill tab will move to the top of the stack.

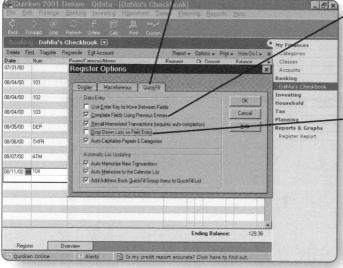

5. Click on the **check marks** next to those options that you do not want to use. The check marks will be removed from these check boxes.

6. Click on the **check boxes** next to those options that you want to use. Check marks will appear in these check boxes.

7. Click on **OK**. The settings you chose will be applied.

NOTE

Click on the Help button to find out what task an option performs.

Working with the Memorized Transaction List

When you use the QuickFill feature, you are actually using transactions that appear in the Memorized Transaction List. This list can be customized so that it is easier to work with the QuickFill feature.

Adding Transactions to the List

A frequently occurring transaction can be added to the Memorized Transaction List. Then, the next time you enter this transaction in the register, the process will be quick and easy.

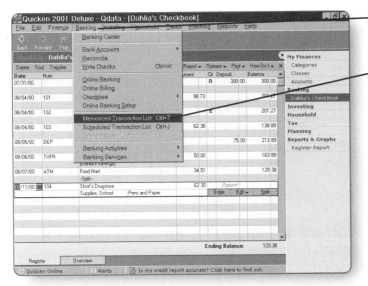

1. **Click** on **Banking**. The Banking menu will appear.

2. **Click** on **Memorized Transaction List**. The Memorized Transaction List window will appear.

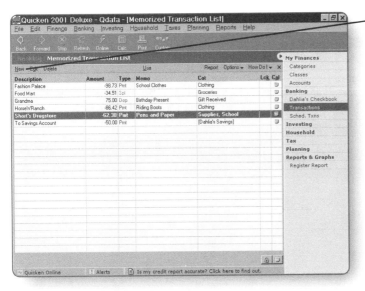

3. **Click** on the **New button**. The Create Memorized Transaction dialog box will open.

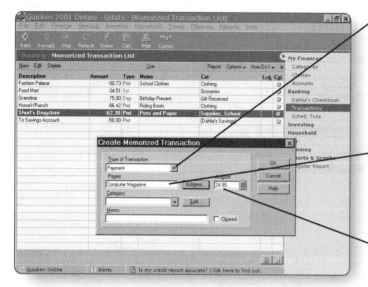

4. **Click** on the **Type of Transaction down arrow** and **click** on the **transaction type** that you want to create. The transaction type will appear in the list box.

5. **Click** in the **Payee text box** and **type** the **name** of the person or business with whom you made the transaction.

6. **Click** in the **Amount text box** and **type** the **amount** of the transaction.

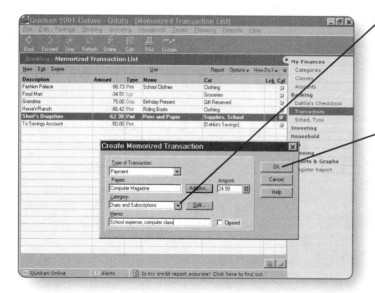

7. **Click** on the **Category down arrow** and **click** on the **category** that applies to the transaction. The category will appear in the list box.

8. **Click** on **OK**. The memorized transaction will appear in the list. You can now access this transaction when you are using the QuickFill feature.

NOTE

If you need to make changes to a memorized transaction, select the transaction from the list and click on the Edit button. You can make your changes in the Edit Memorized Transaction dialog box.

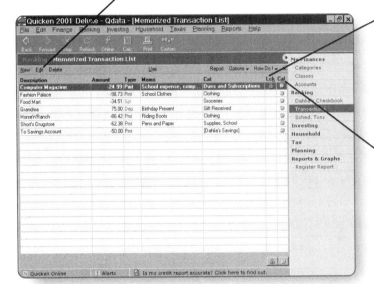

9. Click in the **Lck field** for those transactions that you want updated if you change the transaction when it is recorded in the register. The Lock icon will disappear from the field.

10. Click in the **Cal field** for those transactions that you do not want to appear in the Financial Calendar. The Calendar icon will be removed from the field.

TIP

You'll find the Calendar by opening the Finance menu and selecting Calendar.

Recording Memorized Transactions

Now that you've created a memorized transaction and made changes to the Memorized Transaction List and the QuickFill features to suit your needs, it's time to go to the register and enter the transaction.

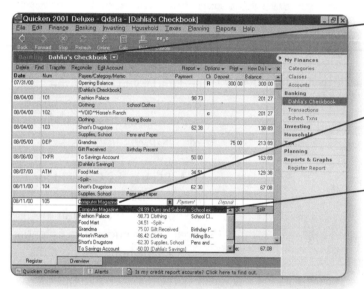

1. Display the **account register** in which you want to record the transaction. The register window will appear.

2. Click in the **Payee field** in a blank transaction line. A drop-down list will appear.

3. Click on the **memorized transaction** that you want to use.

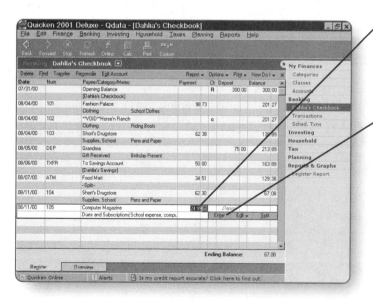

4. Make any **changes** to the transaction, if needed. You may need to add a check number or make a memo to yourself.

5. Click on the **Enter button**. The memorized transaction will be recorded in the register.

7

Reconciling Accounts and Account Statements

Each month you receive a statement for each of your bank, credit card, and investment accounts. Each statement reflects the status and value of your account with a particular financial institution. You'll need to make sure that your records match these statements. Quicken helps you keep track of your accounts and tells you when your records don't match the statements. Your first step is to reconcile the account. After you've compared your Quicken records to the statement, you can run a number of reports to help you locate reconciliation problems. In this chapter, you'll learn how to:

- Reconcile accounts to bank statements
- Create reports to help find reconciliation problems

Balancing Bank Accounts

The purpose of reconciling your accounts is to make sure that each transaction in the register has a match on the bank statement. You'll also want to verify that any canceled checks that are mailed with the statement are recorded correctly on the statement.

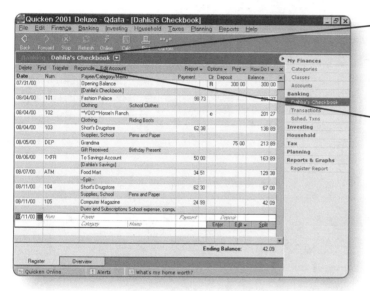

1. **Display** the **account** that you want to reconcile. The account register window will appear.

2. **Click** on the **Reconcile button**. The Reconcile Bank Statement dialog box will open.

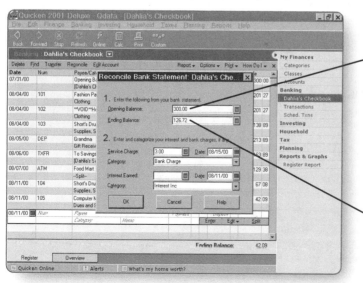

TIP

The amount in the Opening Balance text box in the Reconcile Bank Statement dialog box should match the opening balance that appears on the bank statement.

3. **Click** in the **Ending Balance text box** and **type** the **ending balance** as shown on the bank statement.

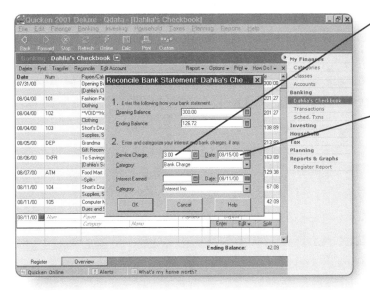

4. Click in the **Service Charge text box** and **type** the **amount** of any fees charged by the bank.

5. Click in the **Date text box** and **type** the **date** the bank charged the fee to your account.

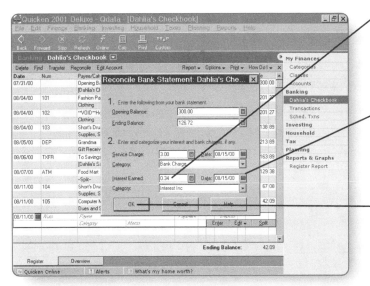

6. Click in the **Interest Earned text box** and **type** the **amount** of any interest income that the bank deposited to your account.

7. Click in the **Date text box** and **type** the **date** the bank deposited the interest to your account.

8. Click on **OK**. The Reconcile Bank Statement window will appear.

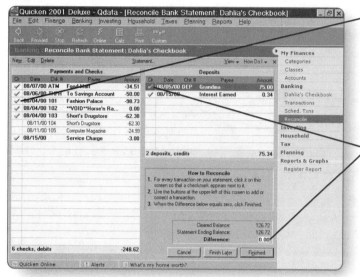

9. Click in the **Clr field** for the checks, cash machine withdrawals, and other payments that appear on the bank statement. A check mark will appear in the field.

10. Click in the **Clr field** for those deposits that appear on the bank statement. A check mark will appear in the field. As you check off each withdrawal and deposit, the amount in the Difference field will change. When this amount is zero, the account is balanced.

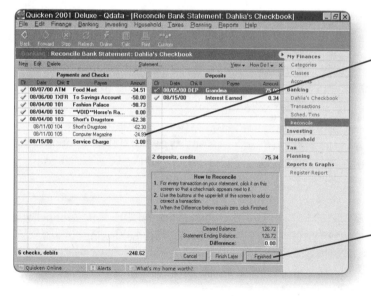

NOTE

If you entered a wrong amount for a transaction, double-click on the entry to display the register. You can edit the register and then return to the Reconcile Bank Statement window.

11. Click on **Finished**. The Reconciliation Complete dialog box will open. This dialog box gives you the opportunity to print a reconciliation report.

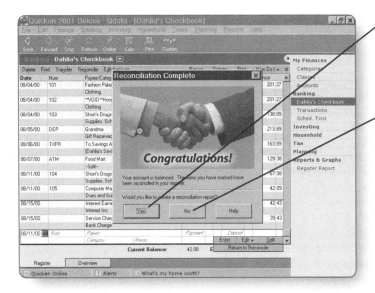

12a. Click on **Yes**. The Reconciliation Report Setup dialog box will open.

OR

12b. Click on **No**. The register window for the account will appear.

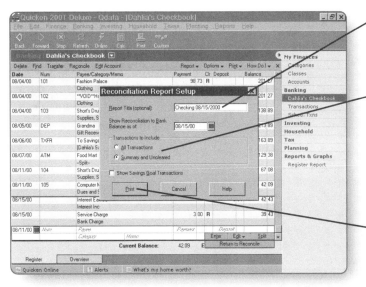

13. Click in the **Report Title (optional) text box** and **type** a **title** for the report.

14. Click on an **option button** in the Transactions to Include section to indicate what transactions you want to display in the report. The option will be selected.

15. Click on **Print**. The Print dialog box will open.

16. **Select** your **print options**. The options will be selected.

17. **Click** on **OK**. The report will print on the selected printer.

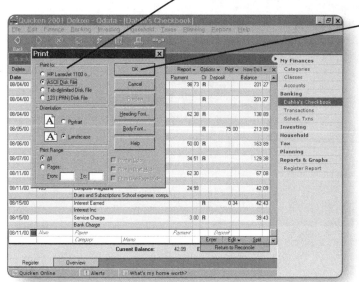

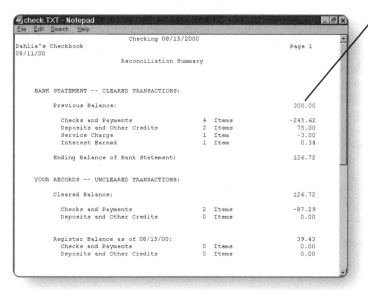

The Reconciliation Summary can be used to compare your records against the bank statement. If your account did not reconcile, look for numbers that are different between your report and the bank statement.

Dealing with Reconciliation Problems

If your account register doesn't balance with your bank statement, you can run several reports in Quicken to help you spot reconciliation problems such as missing checks and duplicate transaction entries.

Creating a Missing Checks Report

The Missing Checks Report lists transactions in the account register by check number. You can easily spot a missing or duplicate check by checking the sequence of the check numbers.

1. Display the **account register** for the account for which you want to create the report. The register window will appear.

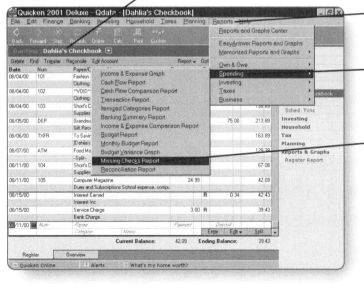

2. Click on **Reports**. The Reports menu will appear.

3. Move the **mouse pointer** to Spending. A submenu will appear.

4. Click on **Missing Checks Report**. The Missing Checks Report window will appear.

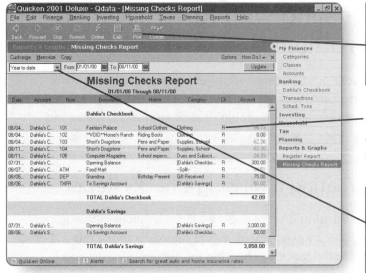

NOTE

You can print the report by clicking on the Print icon.

If the Clr field for a transaction contains an R, that transaction has been reconciled.

TIP

You can customize this report by selecting different report parameters from the drop-down lists in the report window or by clicking on the Options button.

Viewing a Transaction Report

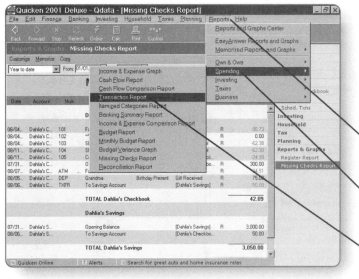

The Transaction Report lists all the transactions in a register. By default, this list is sorted by date, but you can sort transactions by payee, transaction date, or assigned category.

1. Click on **Reports**. The Reports menu will appear.

2. Move the **mouse pointer** to Spending. A submenu will appear.

3. Click on **Transaction Report**. The Transaction Report window will appear.

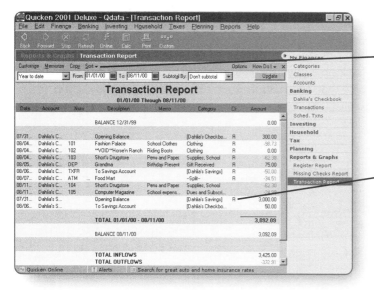

TIP

You can sort the report by clicking on the Sort button. You can sort by date, check number, amount, payee, and category.

The Transaction Report lists all the transactions that you entered during the report period. An R in the Clr column means that a transaction has been reconciled with a bank statement.

Building a Register Report

The Register Report lists all the transactions in an account register. This report comes in handy if you need to keep a paper copy of your checkbook.

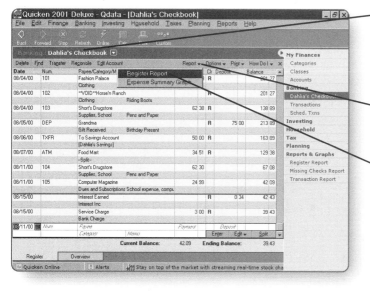

1. Display the **account** for which you want to create a Register Report. The account register window will appear.

2. Click on the **Report button**. A menu will appear.

3. Click on **Register Report**. The Register Report window will appear.

TIP

You can create a report that only lists certain transactions. Click on a payee or category field in a register to display only that information when the Report button is clicked.

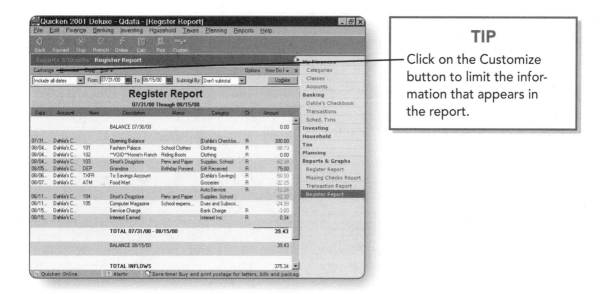

TIP

Click on the Customize button to limit the information that appears in the report.

8

Scheduling Payments

When the monthly bills arrive in the mailbox, most people set them aside to be paid either when they become due or at a time that is more convenient. Quicken can help remind you when to pay your bills. When a bill arrives in the mail, just give Quicken the billing information and you will be reminded when to make the payment. You can also set up Quicken to provide you with other helpful reminders. Quicken can notify you when your checking account reaches a certain minimum balance, when a certificate of deposit matures, or when a customer account becomes past due. In this chapter, you'll learn how to:

- Schedule bills to be paid at a future date
- Pay and record a scheduled transaction
- Create reminders that notify you when an event is about to happen

Creating a Schedule for a Transaction

Quicken can help you remember when to pay your bills. When the bills start showing up in the mailbox, tell Quicken when they need to be paid. Quicken will set up the transaction so that all you need to do is tell Quicken a check number. The rest is done for you.

1. **Click** on **Banking**. The Banking menu will appear.

2. **Click** on **Scheduled Transaction List**. The Scheduled Transaction List window will appear.

NOTE

You can also click on the Sched. Txns QuickTab, if it is displayed.

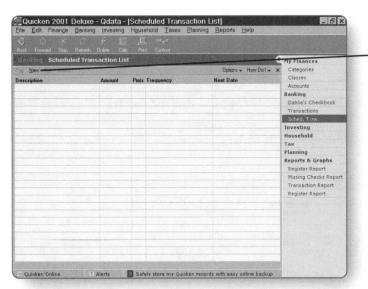

3. **Click** on the **New button**. The Edit Scheduled Transaction dialog box will open.

4. Click on the **Type of Transaction down arrow** and **click** on the **type of transaction**. The transaction type will appear in the list box.

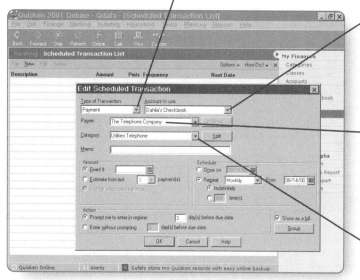

5. Click on the **Account to use down arrow** and **click** on the **account** to which the transaction should be recorded. The account will appear in the list box.

6. Click in the **Payee text box** and **type** the **name** of the person or business to which the transaction applies. You can also use the drop-down list, if needed.

7. Click on the **Category down arrow** and **click** on the **category** to which the transaction should be applied. The category will appear in the list box.

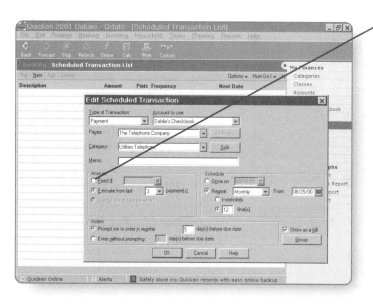

8a. Click on the **Fixed $ option button** in the Amount section if the amount of the transaction stays the same. In the text box, **type** the **amount** to be recorded in the register. The option will be selected and the amount will appear in the text box.

OR

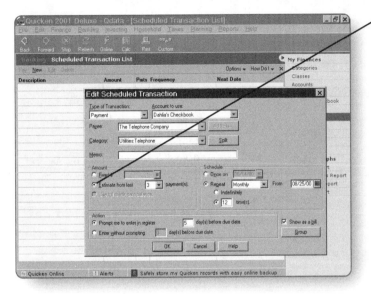

8b. Click on the **Estimate from last option button** if you want to use an average of recent transaction amounts. **Click** on the **payment(s) down arrow** to select the number of previous payments to use to determine the transaction amount. The options will be selected.

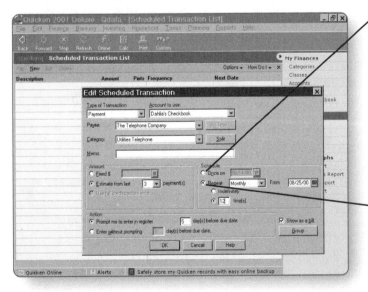

9a. Click on the **Once on option button** in the Schedule section if you only want to schedule one occurrence of the transaction. In the text box, **enter** the **date** on which the transaction is to occur. The option will be selected.

OR

9b. Click on the **Repeat option button** if the transaction is a recurring item. **Select** the **frequency** of the transaction, the **date** on which the first transaction is to occur, and the **number** of times the transaction is to be scheduled. The options will be selected.

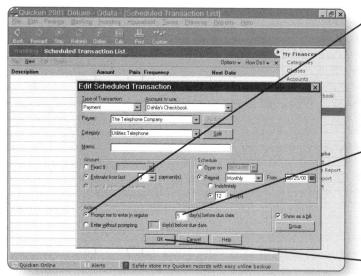

10. **Click** on the **Prompt me to enter in register option button** in the Action section. This option will remind you in advance to record the transaction in the account register.

11. **Click** in the **day(s) before due date text box** and **type** the **number** of days in advance that you want to be reminded that the transaction is becoming due.

12. **Click** on **OK**. The new scheduled transaction will appear in the Scheduled Transaction List.

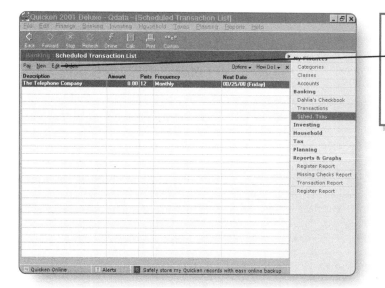

NOTE

If you need to make any changes to this transaction, select it and click on the Edit button.

Paying and Recording a Scheduled Transaction

Once you've scheduled a transaction, it's easy to make the payment. When you open Quicken on those days when you are to be notified of a scheduled transaction, the Quicken Alerts page displays. Here's how you can pay your bills from the Quicken Alerts page.

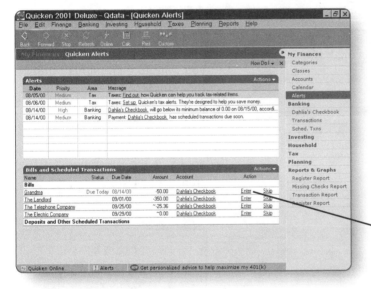

> **NOTE**
>
> You can view the Quicken Alerts page at any time. Open the Finance menu and select Alerts.

1. Click on the **Enter link** next to the transaction that you want to record. The Enter Scheduled Transaction in Register dialog box will open.

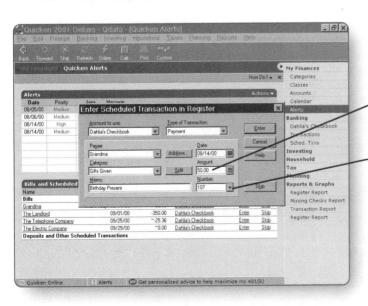

2. Make any **changes** to the transaction, if needed.

3. Type the **amount** of the transaction in the Amount text box.

4. Select the **payment or deposit method** from the Number drop-down list. The option will be selected.

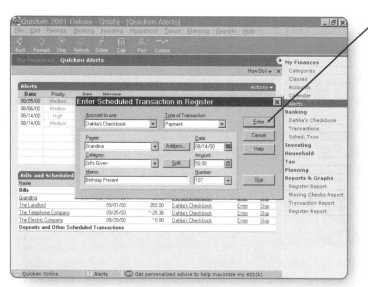

5. Click on **Enter**. The transaction will be recorded in the register for the selected account and you will be returned to the Quicken Alerts page.

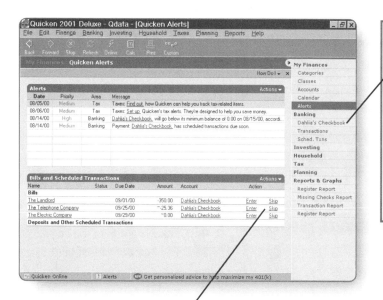

NOTE

Open the register in which the scheduled transaction was recorded to see the recorded transaction. The quickest way to view the register is to click on the account name under the Banking QuickTab.

If the transaction was scheduled to occur just once, you'll notice that the transaction has been removed from the list of bills. If it is a recurring transaction, the Due Date column for the transaction will change to show the next due date for the scheduled transaction.

Creating Alerts

Quicken can be told to notify you when a variety of events are about to occur. You may want to be notified when your checking account reaches a certain maximum amount so that

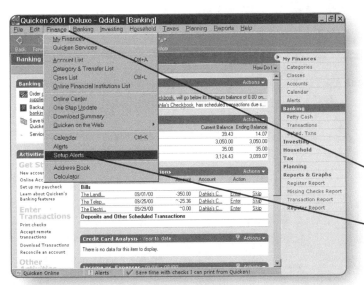

you can transfer this excess money to your savings account. You can remind yourself to reevaluate your insurance policies on an annual basis. And, you can remind yourself to make those quarterly tax payments, if needed.

1. **Click** on **Finance**. The Finance menu will appear.

2. **Click** on **Setup Alerts**. The Set Up Alerts dialog box will open.

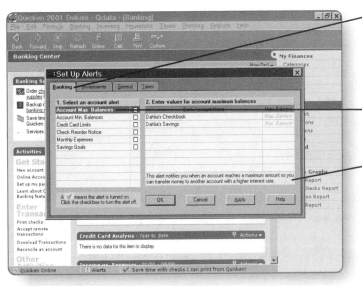

3. **Click** on a **tab**. There are four different categories of alerts from which you can choose.

4. **Click** on an **item** in the Select an account alert list.

5. **Read** the **description** of the alert.

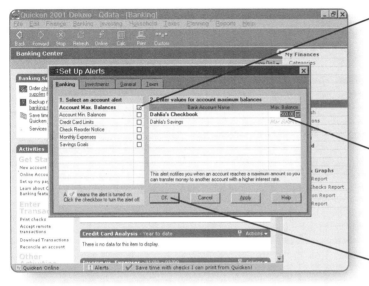

6. Click in the **check box** for the alert that you want to enable. A check mark will appear in the box and you will be prompted to enter the information needed by the alert.

7. Click in the **text box** and **type** the **information** needed by the alert. You may need to set a date, a dollar limit, or some other parameter.

8. Click on **OK**. The alert will be added to the Alerts list.

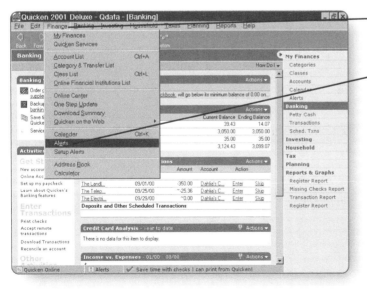

9. Click on **Finance**. The Finance menu will appear.

10. Click on **Alerts**. The Quicken Alerts page will appear.

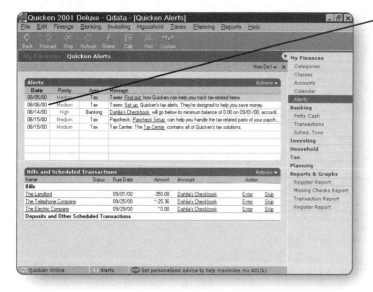

The Quicken Alerts page shows you notifications of important events and when your bills become due. Experiment with scheduled transactions and alerts to help take some of the hassle out of paying your bills. Let Quicken deal with the stress and strain of juggling the checking account.

Part II Review Questions

1. How do you record checks that you've written in the register? *See "Recording a Check Payment" in Chapter 5*

2. How do you transfer money from one account to another account? *See "Transferring Funds between Accounts" in Chapter 5*

3. What information will you find in the Register Report? *See "Printing a Register Report" in Chapter 5*

4. Which Quicken feature automatically completes transaction information in the register? *See "Using QuickFill to Enter Transactions" in Chapter 6*

5. When should you add a transaction to the Memorized Transaction List? *See "Working with the Memorized Transaction List" in Chapter 6*

6. What is the first thing you should do when your bank statements arrive in the mail? *See "Balancing Bank Accounts" in Chapter 7*

7. Which Quicken reports will help you find reconciliation problems between your records and the bank statement? *See "Dealing with Reconciliation Problems" in Chapter 7*

8. Where can you set reminders for yourself so that you pay your bills when they are due? *See "Creating a Schedule for a Transaction" in Chapter 8*

9. How are you notified when a scheduled transaction has become due? *See "Paying and Recording a Scheduled Transaction" in Chapter 8*

10. How can you notify yourself when your bank balance hits an uncomfortable minimum? *See "Creating Alerts" in Chapter 8*

PART III

Working with Special Transactions

9

Watching Pocket Cash

There are many times when you can't use a check or a credit card to pay for your purchases. In these instances, you'll need to pay in cash. You can easily create an account for the money that you withdraw from your accounts in case you need to keep track of your cash spending. Once you have created this petty cash account, you can provide the information for each purchase you made in the petty cash register. To make it easy to remember where you spent your pocket change, save the receipts from your purchases or make a note on a scrap of paper. In this chapter, you'll learn how to:

- Set up a cash account
- Deposit cash into the petty cash account
- Record purchases made with cash out of your pocket

Creating a Petty Cash Account

Before you can begin keeping track of how you spend the cash you withdraw from the cash machine, you must create a petty cash account. To create a petty cash account, you'll need to start from the Account List page. You can get there by selecting Finance, Account List.

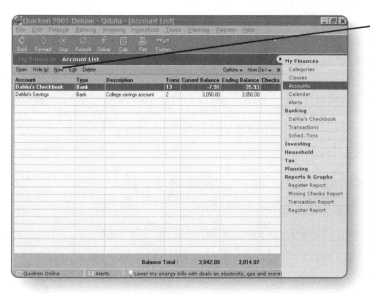

1. **Click** on the **New button**. The Create New Account wizard will start and display the Choose the type of account to create page.

TIP

You can use the keyboard to start the Create New Account wizard. Simply press Ctrl+N.

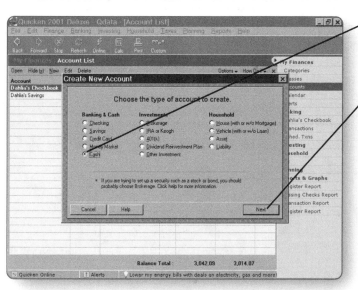

2. **Click** on the **Cash option button**. The option will be selected.

3. **Click** on **Next**. The Enter a name and optional description for this account page will appear.

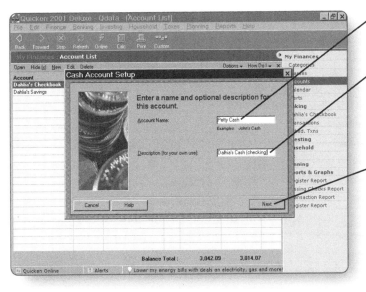

4. Click in the **Account Name text box** and **type Petty Cash**.

5. Click in the **Description (for your own use) text box** and **type** the **purpose** for the account.

6. Click on **Next**. The Enter the starting point information page will appear.

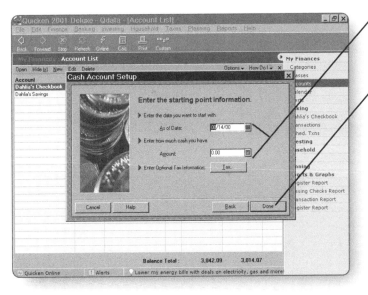

7. Use the **default information** and start with a zero balance in the petty cash account.

8. Click on **Done**. The petty cash account will be added to the list.

NOTE

To view the register for the Cash account you just created, double-click on the account name in the Account List.

Putting Money in the Petty Cash Drawer

To start your petty cash account, just use your ATM card or write a check for cash. When you record the cash withdrawal, show the cash as being transferred to the petty cash account. Here's how to record the transaction in a bank account. Before you begin, open the register for the bank account from which you withdrew the money.

1. Click in the **Date field** and **type** the **date** of the transaction.

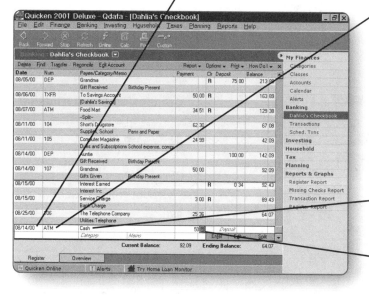

2a. Click in the **Num field** and **type** the **number** of the check that you wrote for cash.

OR

2b. Click the **Num field down arrow** and **click** on **ATM** if you withdrew money from an automated teller machine.

3. Click in the **Payee field** and **type Cash**.

4. Click in the **Payment field** and **type** the **amount** of the cash removed from the account.

5. Click on the **Category field down arrow** and **click** on **Transfer to/from...[Petty Cash]**.

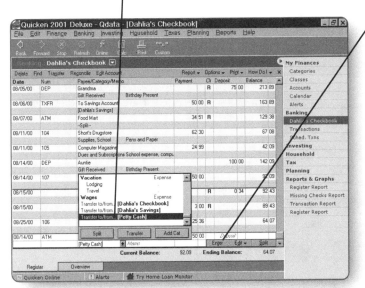

6. Click on **Enter**. The amount of the cash withdrawal will be deducted from the bank account and will appear in the Petty Cash account.

TIP

Initially, the register displays transactions in date order. You can sort transactions in a different order by clicking on a column heading. To sort transactions by check number, click on Num. To view transactions in the order they occurred, click on Date.

Recording Cash Purchases

When you spend the cash that you are carrying around in your pocket, you'll want to keep track of it. You can either make a note to yourself or save the receipt. Then, when you return to Quicken, you can record your cash purchases.

1. **Click** on **Banking**. The Banking menu will appear.

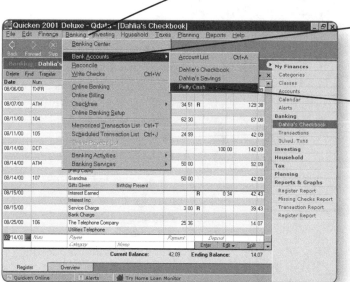

2. **Move** the **mouse pointer** to Bank Accounts. A second menu will appear.

3. **Click** on **Petty Cash**. The Petty Cash account register will appear.

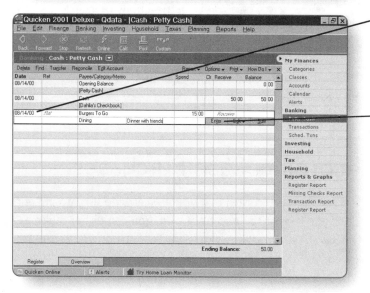

4. **Enter** the **transaction information** for each item for which you spent money out of your pocket.

5. **Click** on the **Enter button**. The cash transaction will be recorded.

10

Recording Your Paycheck

It's easy to track your paycheck as a deposit and just categorize the income. But, if you want to track the paycheck as well as the deductions, use the Paycheck Setup wizard to guide you through the process. You can then automatically record the deposit each payday. You might even want to keep track of unemployment compensation for tax purposes, should that unfortunate event occur. If you have vacation, comp time, or sick leave that you want to track, you can set up a non-monetary account. In this chapter, you'll learn how to:

- Keep track of payroll information automatically
- Record unemployment compensation
- Create and use nonmonetary accounts

Setting Up Your Paycheck

There's a lot of information to record when you deposit your paycheck. Not only do you need to categorize the income, but there are also tax deductions and retirement deductions to consider. The Paycheck Setup wizard will walk you through the process. When you're ready to deposit your next paycheck, take a few minutes to give Quicken the information it needs to easily track your payroll tax information. This section will show you how to get started with the Paycheck Setup wizard.

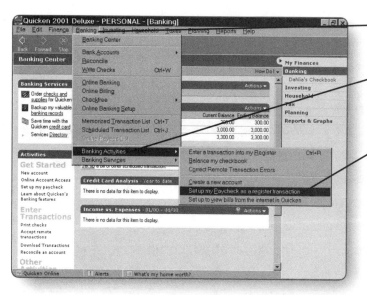

1. Click on **Banking**. The Banking menu will appear.

2. Move the **mouse pointer** to Banking Activities. A submenu will appear.

3. Click on **Set up my Paycheck as a register transaction**. The Paycheck Setup wizard will begin and the Welcome to PayCheck Setup screen will appear.

NOTE

You can also find the Paycheck Setup wizard in the Activities section of the Banking QuickTab.

4. Read the **instructions** on each page. You will be prompted to enter information in text boxes and select options from option buttons and check boxes.

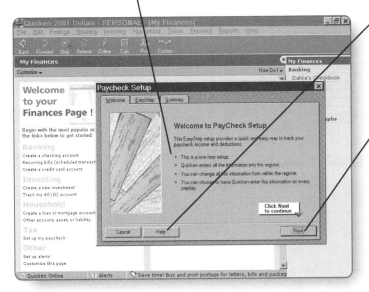

5. Click on **Help** if you need further instructions on how to complete the information requested in a screen. A Help window will appear.

6. Click on **Next**. The Which parts of your paycheck do you want to track? screen will appear.

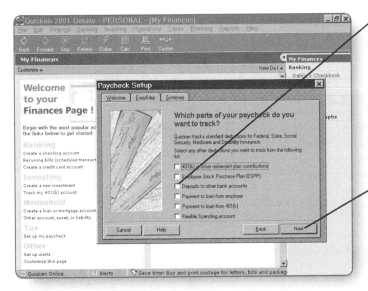

7. Select the **items** from the list that are deducted from your paycheck. A check mark next to an option means that the item is deducted from your paycheck. A cleared check box means that you do not pay for the item as a paycheck deduction.

8. Click on **Next**. The Create a name and enter how often you receive your paycheck screen will appear.

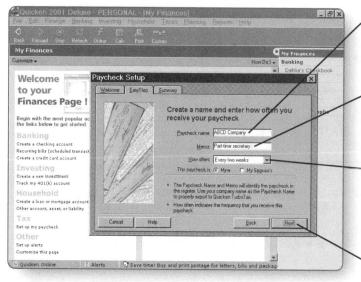

9. **Click** in the **Paycheck name text box** and **type** the **name** of your employer.

10. **Click** in the **Memo field** and **type** a **description** of your job.

11. **Click** on the **How often down arrow** and **select how often** you receive a paycheck. The option will be selected.

12. **Click** on **Next**. The Enter your most current paycheck information screen will appear.

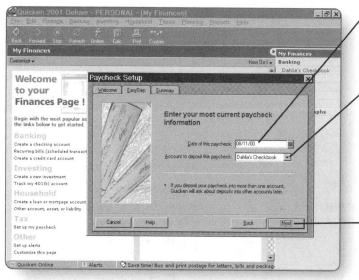

13. **Click** in the **Date of this paycheck field** and **type** the **date** you received the paycheck.

14. **Click** on the **Account to deposit this paycheck down arrow** and **select** the **account** into which you will deposit your paycheck. The account will be selected.

15. **Click** on **Next**. The Enter the gross and net amounts of your paycheck screen will appear.

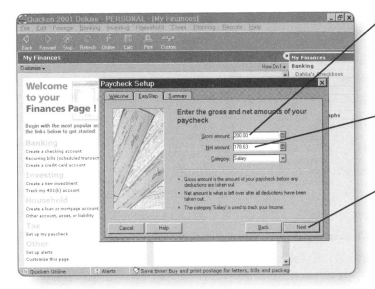

16. Click in the **Gross amount text box** and **type** the **amount** of your wages before taxes and other deductions.

17. Click in the **Net amount text box** and **type** the **amount** of the check.

18. Click on **Next**. The Are there any other sources of income for this paycheck? screen will appear.

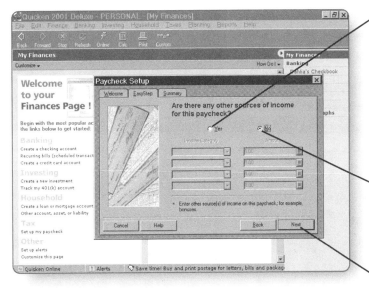

19a. Click on the **Yes option button** if the paycheck contains income other than your regular salary. The option will be selected. Select categories for the other sources of income and type the amount of each.

OR

19b. Click on the **No option button** if your salary is the only income source. The option will be selected.

20. Click on **Next**. The Enter the standard tax deductions taken out of your paycheck screen will appear.

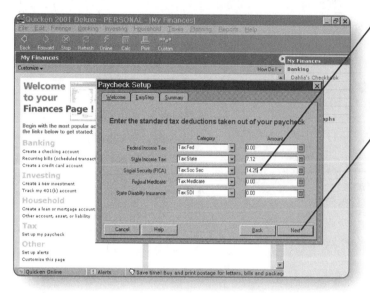

21. In the Amount column, **click** in the **text box** next to each type of tax that is deducted from your paycheck and **type** the **amount** of the tax deduction.

22. Click on **Next** when you are finished. The Are there any other taxes to be taken out of your paycheck? screen will appear.

23a. Click on the **Yes option button** if the paycheck contains other tax deductions. The option will be selected. Select categories for the other tax deductions and type the amount of each.

OR

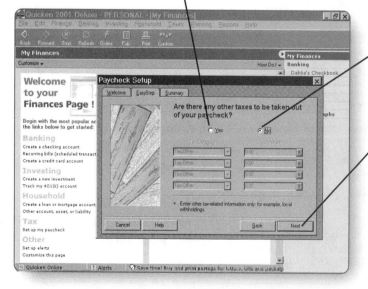

23b. Click on the **No option button** if there are no other tax deductions. The option will be selected.

24. Click on **Next**. The Are there any other deductions listed on your paycheck? screen will appear.

NOTE

You may see additional screens. The screens that display during the wizard will vary depending on the deductions you selected on the Which parts of your paycheck do you want to track? screen.

25a. **Click** on the **Yes option button** if the paycheck contains other deductions. The option will be selected. Select categories for the other deductions and type the amount of each.

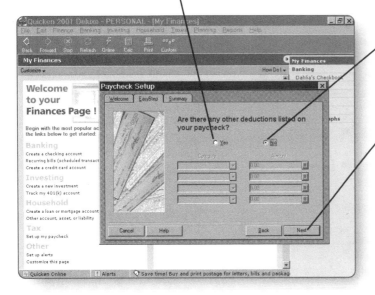

OR

25b. **Click** on the **No option button** if there are no other deductions. The option will be selected.

26. **Click** on **Next**. The Quicken will record this information in your account screen will appear.

27a. **Click** on the **Yes option button** if you want Quicken to automatically remind you to enter your paycheck. Selecting this option will set up the transaction in the Scheduled Transaction List. The option will be selected.

OR

27b. **Click** on the **No option button** if you don't want Quicken to automatically remind you to enter your paycheck. Selecting this option will set up the transaction in the Memorized Transaction List. The option will be selected.

28. **Click** on **Next**. The You're done! screen will appear.

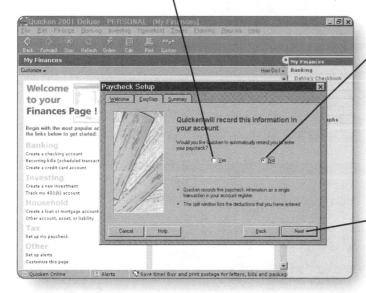

29. **Verify** that the **information** you entered is correct.

30. **Click** on **Done**. The transaction will be recorded in the selected account register. Also, the deposit will be remembered as a memorized or a scheduled transaction. You can use this memorized or scheduled transaction the next time you need to deposit your paycheck.

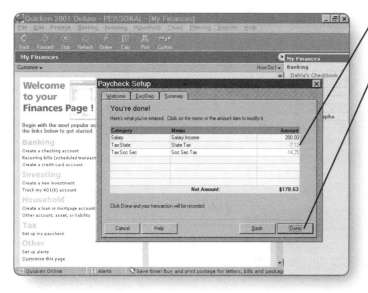

> **TIP**
>
> You learned how to work with the Memorized Transaction List in Chapter 6, "Automating Transactions," and how to use the Scheduled Transaction List in Chapter 8, "Scheduling Payments."

Entering Unemployment Checks

If you find yourself unemployed, Quicken can help with some of the burden by recording unemployment benefits. Depending on how much other income you earn during the year, you may have to declare the unemployment earnings at tax time.

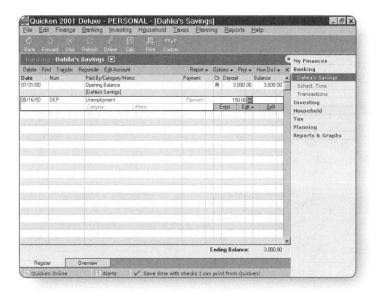

> **NOTE**
>
> Before you begin, you need to make sure that a category called Unemployment Inc appears in the Category & Transfer List. If this category is not listed, you'll need to add the category. See Chapter 4, "Creating a Chart of Accounts."

1. Display the **register window** for the account into which you deposited the unemployment check. The register will appear.

2. In the Date field, **type** the **date** that you deposited the unemployment check.

3. Click in the **Num field** to display a drop-down list and **click** on **Deposit**. DEP will appear in the Num field.

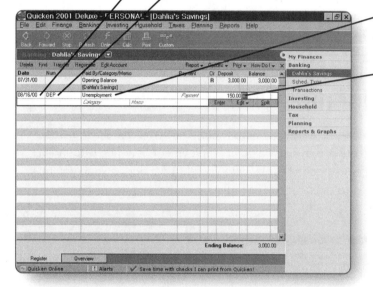

4. Click in the **Payee field** and **type** a **description**.

5. Click in the **Deposit field** and **type** the **amount** of the unemployment check.

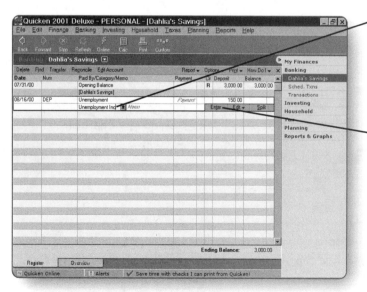

6. Click in the **Category field**. The list of categories will appear.

7. Click on **Unemployment Inc**. The category will be selected.

8. Click on the **Enter button**. The deposit will be recorded in your account and the unemployment income will be recorded in the appropriate category.

TIP

Save time and mouse clicks when selecting a category. Type the first few letters of the category name and the Category list box will automatically display the list item that most closely matches the letters that were typed.

Keeping Track of Vacation Time

You can keep track of how much vacation time you've earned and how much vacation time you've used. You can also keep track of accumulated sick leave. You don't have to limit these nonmonetary accounts to just employment-related items.

Creating a Nonmonetary Account

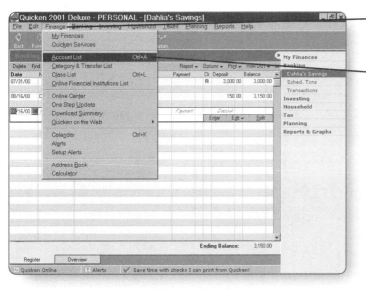

1. **Click** on **Finance**. The Finance menu will appear.

2. **Click** on **Account List**. The Account List window will appear.

NOTE

If you've used this list before, you can click on the Accounts QuickTab.

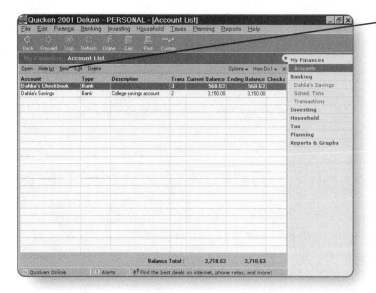

3. Click on the **New button**. The Create New Account wizard will start and the Choose the type of account to create screen will appear.

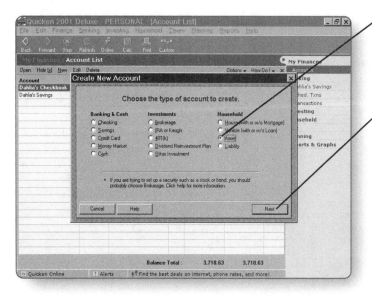

4. Click on the **Asset option button** in the Household category. The option will be selected.

5. Click on **Next**. The Asset Account Setup wizard will start and the Enter a name and optional description for this account screen will appear.

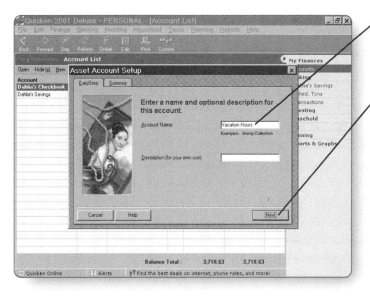

6. Type a **name** for the nonmonetary account in the Account Name text box.

7. Click on **Next**. The Enter the starting point information screen will appear.

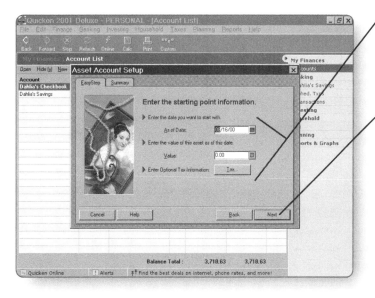

8. Accept the **default information**. The current date will be used and the account will start with a zero balance.

9. Click on **Next** to display the Summary screen.

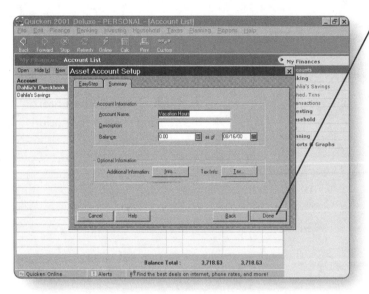

10. **Click** on **Done** after you have verified that the information is correct. The nonmonetary account will be added to the Account List.

Recording Vacation Hours

Once the nonmonetary account is created, you can begin keeping track of nonmonetary items.

1. **Click** on the **nonmonetary account** that you want to use. The account will be selected.

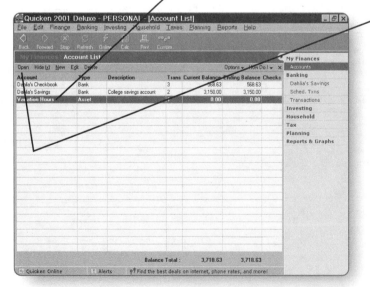

2. **Click** on the **Open button**. The register window for the nonmonetary account will appear.

3. Click in the **Date field** and **type** the **date** on which the nonmonetary transaction was made. The date will appear in the Date field.

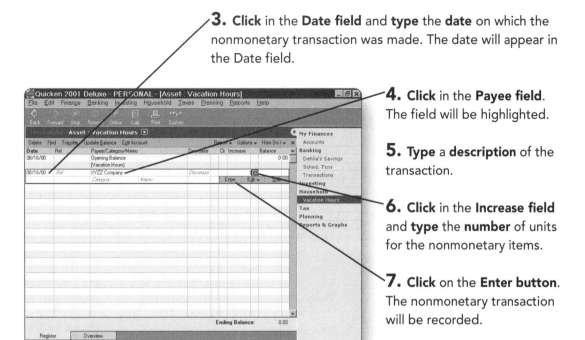

4. Click in the **Payee field**. The field will be highlighted.

5. Type a **description** of the transaction.

6. Click in the **Increase field** and **type** the **number** of units for the nonmonetary items.

7. Click on the **Enter button**. The nonmonetary transaction will be recorded.

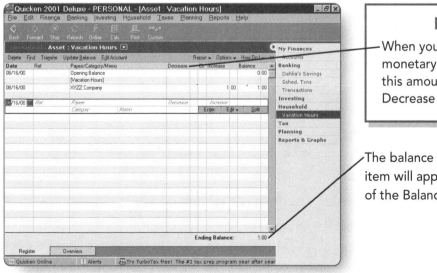

NOTE

When you use your non-monetary items, enter this amount in the Decrease field.

The balance of the nonmonetary item will appear in the last row of the Balance field.

11

Creating Mortgage Accounts

One of the biggest purchases you might make during your lifetime is a home. Quicken includes features that help you keep track of the mortgage payments and the value of your home. Because there's a lot involved in a mortgage payment (such as principal reduction, interest payments, and deposits and payments to an escrow account), it's worth the time to set up a special way to handle this type of loan. In this chapter, you'll learn how to:

- Set up a mortgage loan account
- Make payments on your mortgage
- Produce mortgage and home equity reports

Setting Up a Mortgage Account

After you get moved into your new house and have the furniture in place, you'll need to find an easy way to keep track of your mortgage and interest payments. Use the Quicken Loan Setup wizard to create an account for the mortgage. You can also set up an asset account to help keep track of the value of your home. If you have a variable interest rate loan, Quicken can automatically adjust the mortgage information.

Creating a Mortgage Loan Account

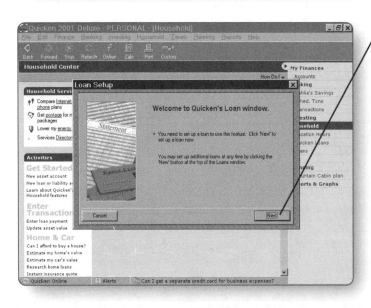

1. Click on **Household**. The Household menu will appear.

2. Click on **Loans**. The Loan Setup wizard will start.

3. Click on the **Next button**. The EasyStep Setup will begin.

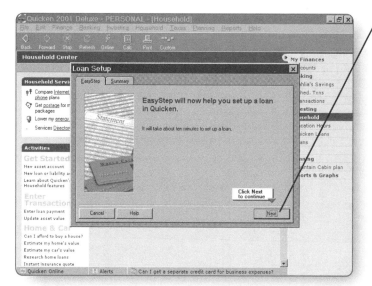

4. Click on **Next**. The What type of loan is this? page will appear.

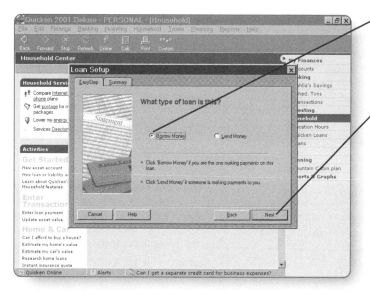

5. Click on the **Borrow Money option button**, if it is not already selected. The option will be selected.

6. Click on **Next**. The Choose a Quicken account for this loan page will appear.

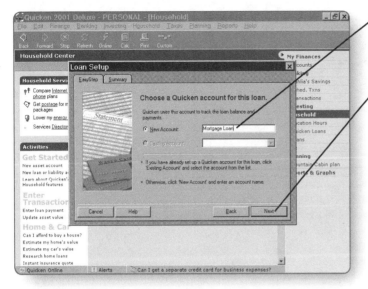

7. Click in the **New Account text box** and **type** a **name** for the loan account.

8. Click on **Next**. The Have any payments been made on this loan? page will appear.

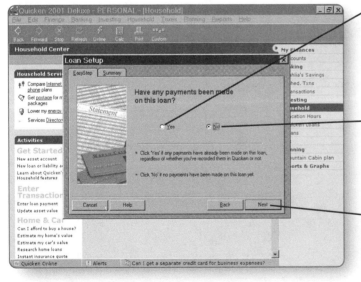

9a. Click on the **Yes option button** if payments have been made on this loan. The option will be selected.

OR

9b. Click on the **No option button** if you have not made any payments on this loan. The option will be selected.

10. Click on **Next**. The Enter the initial loan information screen will appear.

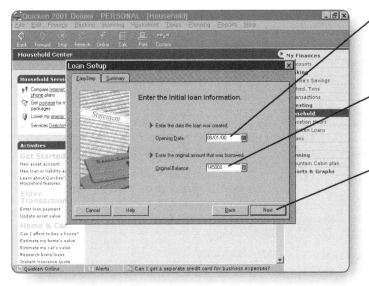

11. Click in the **Opening Date text box** and **type** the **date** on which you took out the loan.

12. Click in the **Original Balance text box** and **type** the **original amount** of the loan.

13. Click on **Next**. The Does this loan include a balloon payment at the end? page will appear.

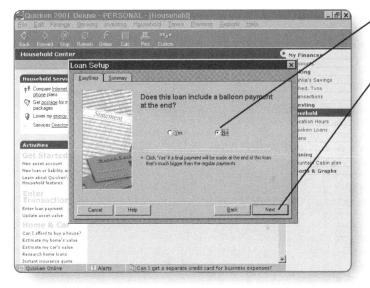

14. Click on an **option button**. The option will be selected.

15. Click on **Next**. The Enter the original length of the loan page will appear.

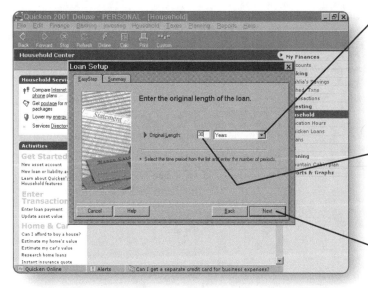

16. Click on the **Original Length down arrow** and **click** on the **time period** used to determine the length of the loan. The time period will be selected.

17. Click in the **Original Length text box** and **type** the **number** of time periods needed to pay off the loan.

18. Click on **Next**. The Enter the payment period for this loan page will appear.

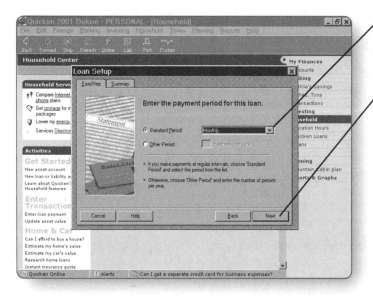

19. Select the **frequency** at which you make loan payments. The option will be selected.

20. Click on **Next**. The Enter the compounding period for this loan page will appear.

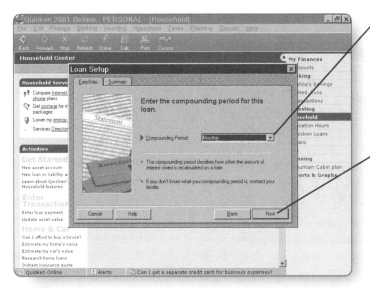

21. Click on the **Compounding Period down arrow** and **click** on the **time period** used to calculate compound interest. The compounding period will be selected.

22. Click on **Next**. The Enter the date of the first payment page will appear.

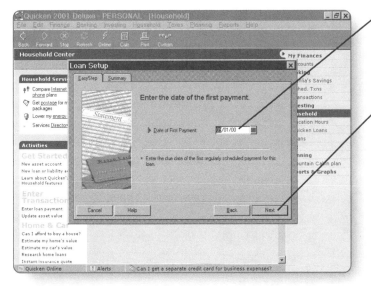

23. Click in the **Date of First Payment text box** and **type** the **date** on which the first payment on the loan is due.

24. Click on **Next**. The Do you know the amount of the first payment? page will appear.

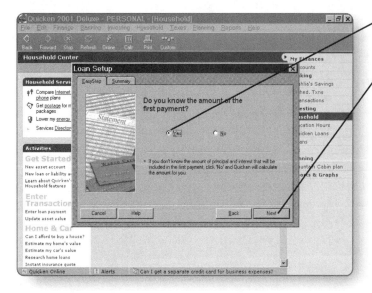

25. **Click** on an **option button**. The option will be selected.

26. **Click** on **Next**. The Enter the amount of principal and interest in the next payment page will appear.

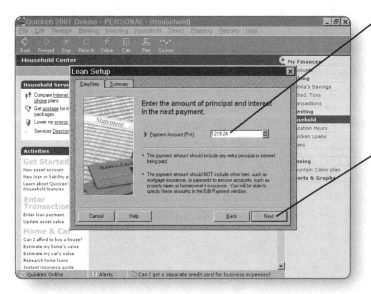

27. **Click** in the **Payment Amount (P+I) text box** and **type** the **amount** of your principal and interest payment as determined by your mortgage lender.

28. **Click** on **Next**. The Enter the interest rate for this loan page will appear.

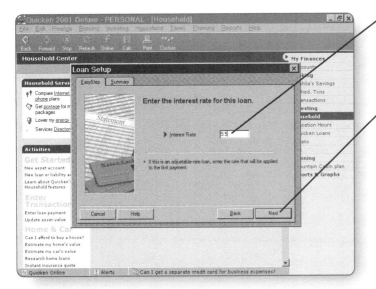

29. **Click** in the **Interest Rate text box** and **type** the **interest rate** that you pay on your mortgage loan.

30. **Click** on **Next**. The Summary page will appear.

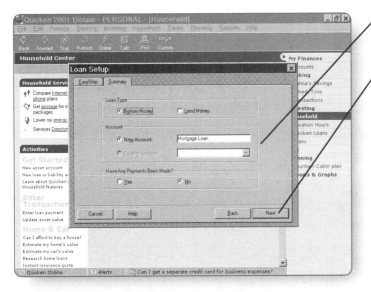

31. **Verify** that the **information** is correct.

32. **Click** on **Next**. Another page of loan information will appear.

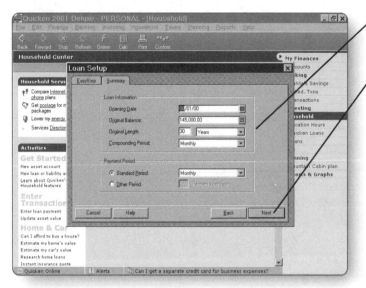

33. Verify that the **information** is correct.

34. Click on **Next**. Another page of loan information will appear.

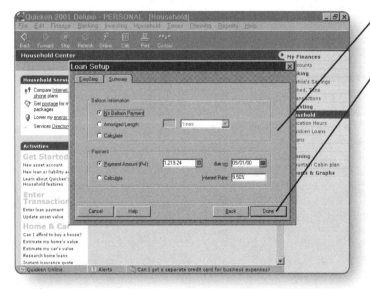

35. Verify that the **information** is correct.

36. Click on **Done**. The Set Up Loan Payment dialog box will open.

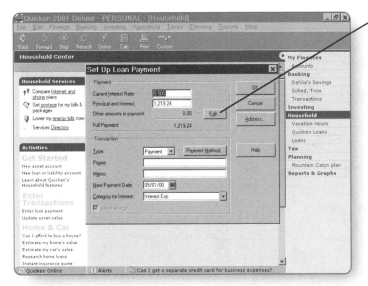

37. **Click** on **Edit**, if there are other amounts that will be added to your mortgage payment. The Split Transaction Window will appear.

NOTE

There may be home-owner's insurance and property tax payments that your mortgage lender pays for you out of an escrow account.

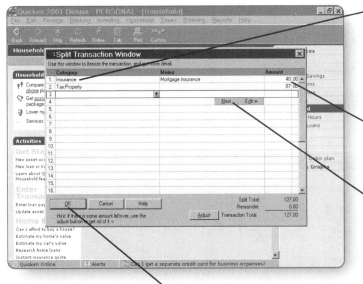

38. **Click** in the **Category field** and **select** the **category** that applies to the additional payment amount. The category will appear in the field.

39. **Click** in the **Amount field** and **type** the **amount** of the additional payment.

40. **Click** on the **Next button**. The second transaction line will be selected. You can add any additional payments in this transaction line.

41. **Click** on **OK**. The Set Up Loan Payment dialog box will open. Notice that the amount in the Full Payment field will change to show the total mortgage payment.

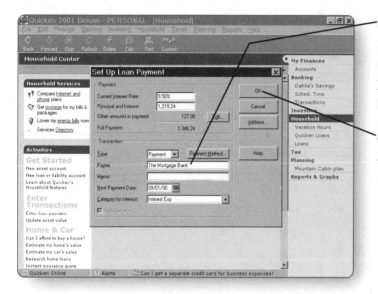

42. Click in the **Payee field** and **type** the **name** of the mortgage lender to whom you will make your mortgage payments.

43. Click on **OK**. A confirmation dialog box will open.

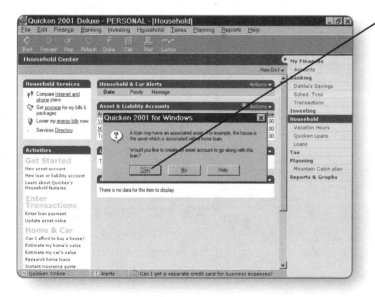

44. Click on **Yes**. The Asset Account Setup wizard will begin.

45. **Click** on the **Summary tab**. The Summary tab will move to the top of the stack.

46. **Click** in the **Account Name text box** and **type** a **name** to describe the home for which you are tracking the mortgage payments.

47. **Click** in the **Balance text box** and **type** the **market value** of the house.

48. **Click** in the **as of text box** and **type** the **date** of the market valuation of the house.

49. **Click** on **Done**. You will return to the View Loans window.

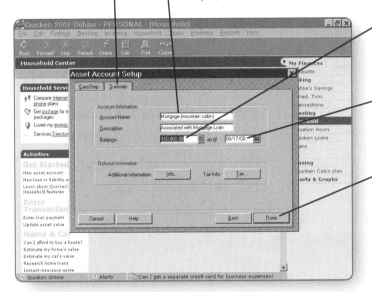

The mortgage loan that you just created will appear in the View Loans window.

NOTE

If you need to make any changes to this loan, click on the Edit Loan button.

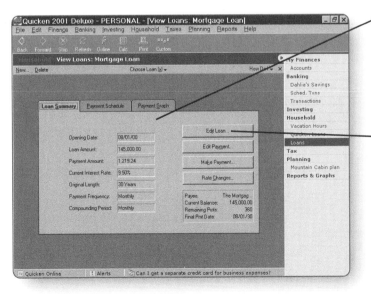

Dealing with Adjustable Rate Loans

Most loans are for a fixed interest rate. If you have an adjustable rate mortgage, you'll need to enter the various interest rate changes and the date those changes go into effect.

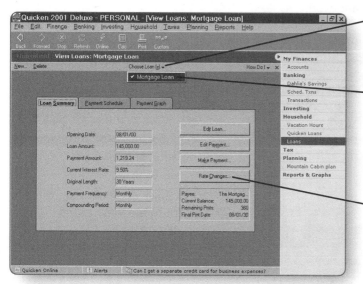

1. Click on the **Choose Loan button**. A list of loans that have been set up will appear.

2. Click on the **mortgage loan** for which you want to change the interest rate. The mortgage loan will appear in the View Loans window.

3. Click on **Rate Changes**. The Loan Rate Changes dialog box will open.

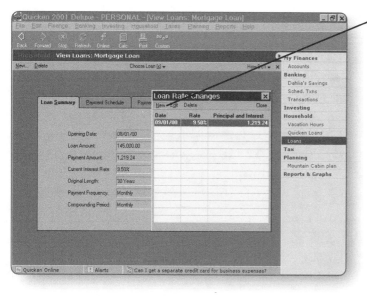

4. Click on the **New button**. The Insert an Interest Rate Change dialog box will open.

5. **Click** in the **Effective Date text box** and **type** the **date** on which the new interest rate will start.

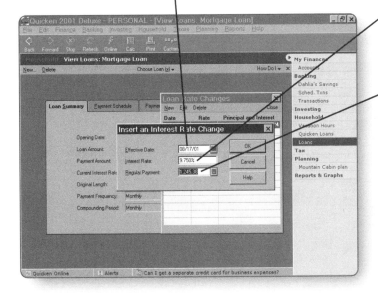

6. **Click** in the **Interest Rate text box** and **type** the **interest rate**.

7. **Click** in the **Regular Payment text box**. The amount of the new payment will appear.

8. **Verify** that the **new payment amount** is correct.

9. **Click** on **OK**. You will return to the Loan Rate Changes dialog box.

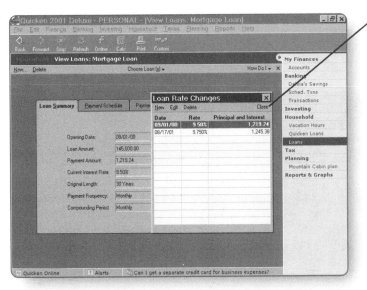

10. **Click** on the **Close button**. The new interest rate and payment will be set up and can be used when the rate changes go into effect.

Recording Mortgage Payments

When it's time to make a mortgage payment, use the payment function in the View Loans window to enter the payment in the proper account register. You can also record extra amounts that you might add to a mortgage payment if you are trying to pay off the loan faster.

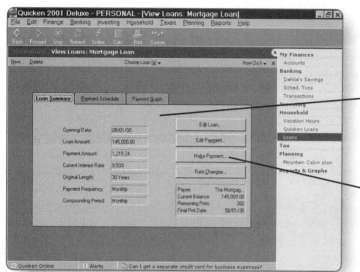

1. In the View Loans window, **display** the **loan** on which you want to make the payment. The loan will appear.

2. Click on **Make Payment**. The Loan Payment dialog box will open.

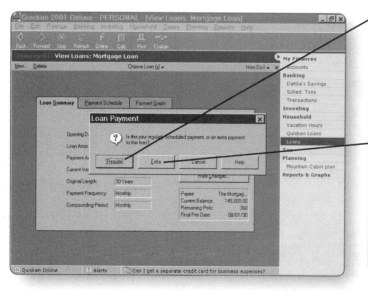

3. Click on **Regular**. The Make Regular Payment dialog box will open.

TIP

To help pay off your mortgage loan faster (and reduce the amount of interest you will pay over the duration of the loan), make an extra payment when you can afford it.

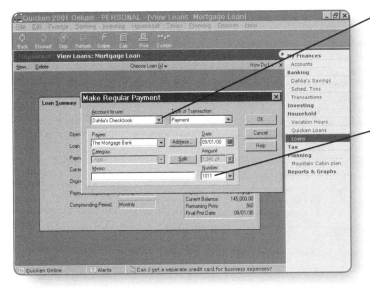

4. **Click** on the **Account to use down arrow** and **click** on the **account** from which you will be making the mortgage payment. The account will be selected.

5. **Click** in the **Number text box** and **type** the **number** of the check you will use to make the payment.

6. **Click** on **OK**. The payment will be recorded in the selected account register.

Producing Mortgage Reports

When you want to find out the balance of your mortgage loan and your home equity, you can produce a couple of reports. The payment schedule will show you how much you have paid in principal and interest and how much is remaining on the mortgage loan. The second report shows you how much equity you have in your home.

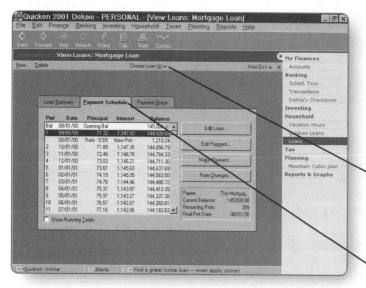

Viewing the Payment Schedule

You can easily see running totals for your principal and interest payments that you've made to date. Simply follow these steps.

1. Display the **loan** for which you want to produce a payment schedule. The loan will appear in the View Loans window.

2. Click on the **Payment Schedule tab**. The Payment Schedule tab will move to the top of the stack.

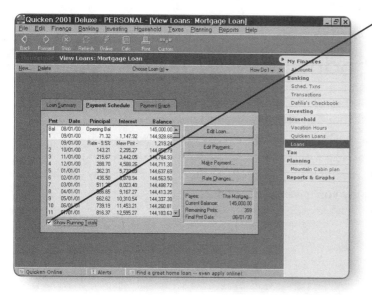

3. Click in the **Show Running Totals check box**. A check mark will appear in the box and the total amount of principal and interest payments you've made to date will be displayed.

Determining Your Home Equity

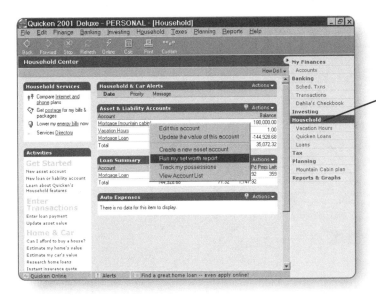

With Quicken, you can easily track your home equity by creating a Net Worth Report.

1. **Click** on the **Household QuickTab**. The Household Center screen will appear.

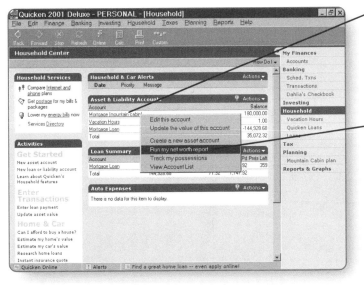

2. **Right-click** on the **asset account** that you created for your house when you set up the mortgage loan. A menu will appear.

3. **Click** on **Run my net worth report**. The Net Worth Report will appear in the Reports & Graphs window.

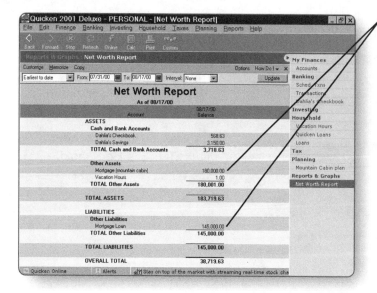

You'll need to customize this report to show only your mortgage loan account and house asset account.

12

Dealing with Taxes

In Chapter 4, "Creating a Chart of Accounts," you learned how to associate a category with a tax form line item. The ability to link your income and spending to a tax category will help make tax time a little simpler. If you are unsure of which income and spending amounts are taxable, Quicken contains a number of tools to help you out. Not only will Quicken link a tax form line item to a category, but Quicken can help you find additional tax deductions and help estimate your tax liability. Make tax time a little less frustrating and let Quicken help you ease the burden of preparing your tax return. In this chapter, you'll learn how to:

- Determine your allowable tax deductions
- Estimate your tax liability
- Prepare reports that you can use at tax time

Finding Tax Deductions

A number of categories are already set up so that amounts recorded in a category are assigned to a tax form and to a line item on that tax form. If you have added new categories, or if a category is not assigned to a tax form, you may need some help associating a tax form line item with a spending category. Quicken contains a number of tools that will help you determine the tax deductions for which you qualify.

Maximizing Your Itemized Deductions

It's hard to keep up with the tax changes and to know what is an allowable deduction on your taxes. If you want to know which itemized deductions (those found on Schedule A) you can claim, take a look at the Itemized Deduction Estimator. The Itemized Deduction Estimator might even help you find some overlooked deductions.

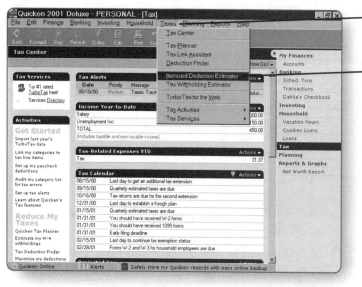

1. Click on **Taxes**. The Taxes menu will appear.

2. Click on **Itemized Deduction Estimator**. The Itemized Deduction Estimator will start.

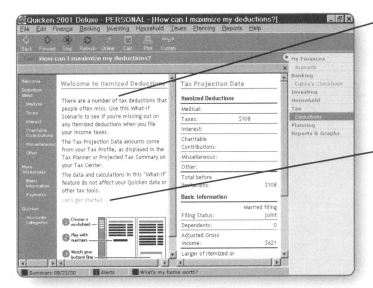

3. **Read** the **instructions** carefully. The Itemized Deduction Estimator will walk you through the process of finding itemized deductions for which you may qualify.

4. **Click** on the **Let's get started link**. The Medical Deductions page will appear.

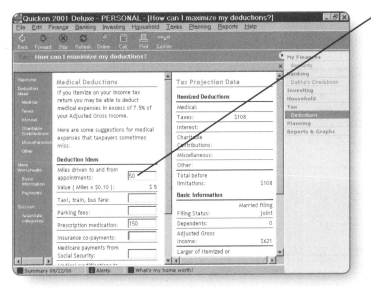

5. **Click** in a **text box** and **type** the requested **information**.

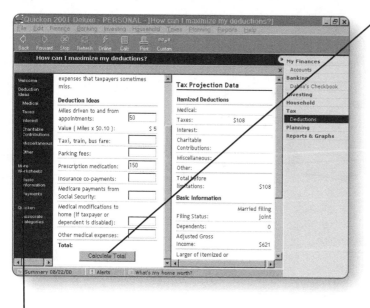

6. **Click** on the **Calculate Total button** at the bottom of the page. The information you typed will appear at the right side of the page.

7. **Click** on the **Taxes link** found at the left side of the page. The Taxes page will appear.

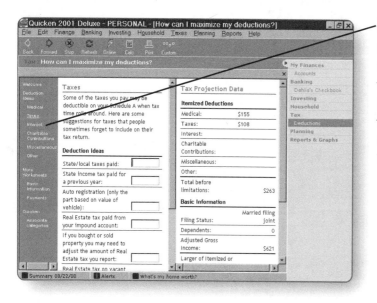

8. **Work** through the **remaining categories** found at the left side of the page. When you get to the end of the Itemized Deduction Estimator, you can then make sure that any tax-related categories are set up in Quicken.

Qualifying for Other Deductions

You can easily tell Quicken which tax form to use for a category. You can also obtain help deciding on an appropriate tax form. It's time to retain the services of the Tax Link Assistant.

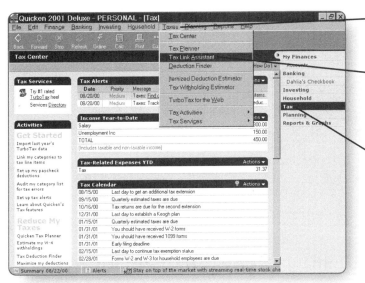

1. Click on **Taxes**. The Taxes menu will appear.

2. Click on **Tax Link Assistant**. The Tax Link Assistant will appear.

> **NOTE**
>
> The Tax Center is a great place to see your tax situation at a glance, keep track of due dates on taxes, find tax-related information on the Web, and find help with tax problems.

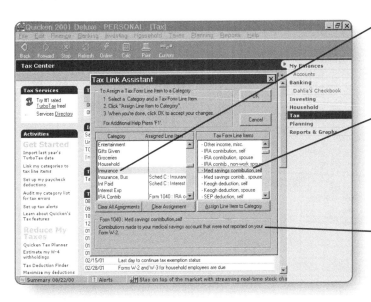

3. In the Category list, **click** on a **category** to which you want to assign a tax form. The category will be selected.

4. In the Tax Form Line Items list, **click** on the **tax form and line item** that you want to apply to the category. The tax form and line item will be selected.

5. Read the **description** of the type of income or expenditures that can be reported on the tax form to determine if the transactions you recorded in the category qualify.

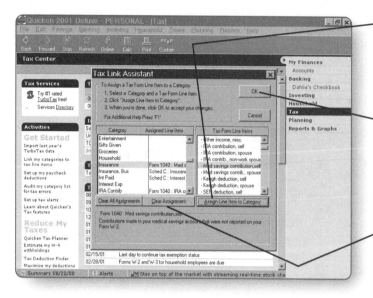

6. Click on the **Assign Line Item to Category button.** The tax form and line item will be assigned to the category.

7. Click on **OK.** The tax form changes will be applied to the category items.

TIP

You can remove a tax form assignment from a category. Click on the category and then click on the Clear Assignment button.

Finding More Tax Deductions

If you're not quite certain about all this tax deduction stuff, you can go to another place to get more information before you begin assigning tax forms to categories. The Deduction Finder is a great tool for reviewing the available deductions and helping you determine if you qualify for the deduction.

1. Click on **Taxes.** The Taxes menu will appear.

2. Click on **Deduction Finder.** The Deduction Finder will appear in the Taxes window and the Introduction to Deduction Finder dialog box will open.

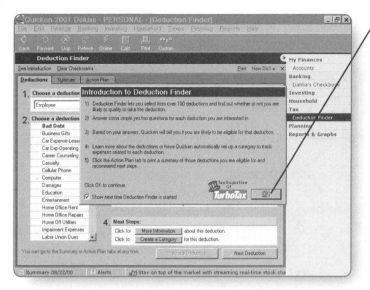

3. Click on **OK**. You can begin working with the Deduction Finder.

4. Click on the **Choose a deduction type down arrow** and **click** on the **type of deduction** for which you are searching. The deduction type will appear in the list box and the list of available deductions for that type will appear in the Choose a deduction list.

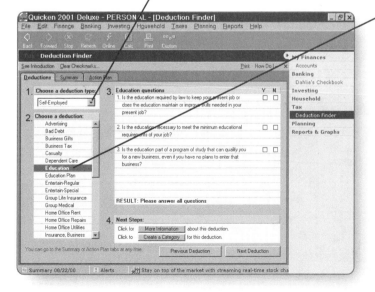

5. Click on the **deduction** for which you want to determine your eligibility. The deduction will be selected and a list of questions will appear that can help you decide if you qualify for the deduction.

NOTE

You may also want to consult a tax specialist. A tax specialist can make sure that you have set up your categories and tax deductions properly.

6. Click in the **Y or N check box** to answer yes or no to each question. A check mark will appear in the selected check box.

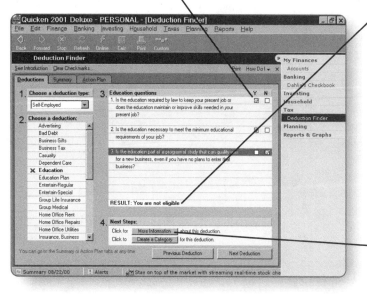

7. Read the **result**. After you answer all the questions, the RESULT line will tell you whether or not you can take the deduction. If you qualify for a deduction, you'll want to know more about the deduction and how Quicken handles it. You'll also need to make sure that you have the appropriate categories set up for the tax deduction.

8. Click on the **More Information button**. A More Information dialog box will open.

The More Information dialog box tells you how Quicken will handle the tax category, and about deduction limits, paperwork requirements, the tax form used, and other information that is pertinent to the deduction.

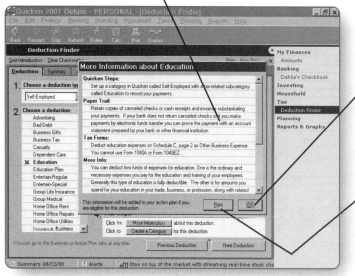

9. Click on **OK**. You will return to the Deduction Finder.

TIP

Keep a copy of this information by clicking on the Print button.

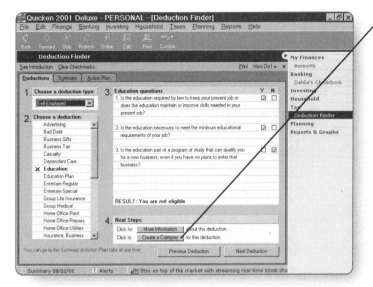

10. **Click** on the **Create a Category button**. The Create a category dialog box will open.

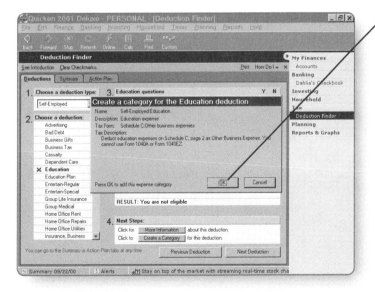

11. **Click** on **OK**. You will return to the Deduction Finder.

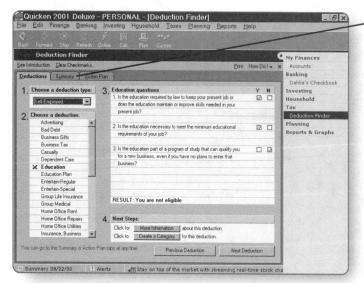

12. Click on the **Summary tab**. The Summary tab will move to the top of the stack.

The Summary tab shows the number of deductions listed for each deduction type, the number of deductions for which you answered questions, and the number of deductions for which you qualify.

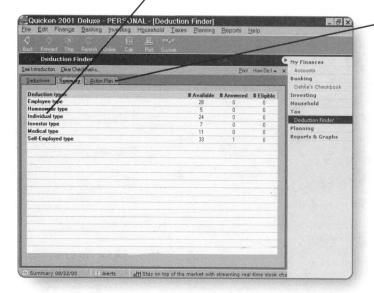

13. Click on the **Action Plan tab**. The Action Plan tab will move to the top of the stack.

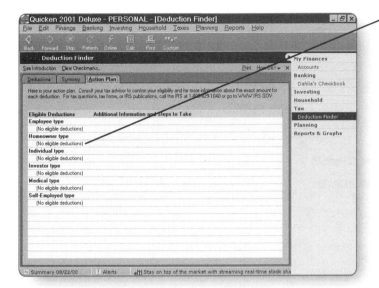

The Action Plan tab provides information about each of the deductions for which you could be eligible. Information such as qualification criteria, deduction limits, and paperwork requirements are detailed.

Estimating Taxes

Quicken provides excellent aids for determining how much you owe in taxes for a given tax period. You'll need to know how much money to set aside for tax payments. Even though the information provided by Quicken is very good, you may want to take your tax information to a tax preparation specialist or use a tax preparation software program such as Intuit's TurboTax.

Locating the Tax Planner

An easy way to determine what you'll owe in taxes is to consult the Tax Planner. The Tax Planner takes the tax information from your Quicken data file and estimates the amount of taxes you owe or your tax refund. You can also use the Tax Planner to play some "What if?" scenarios and see how changes in your income or tax deduction would affect your tax situation.

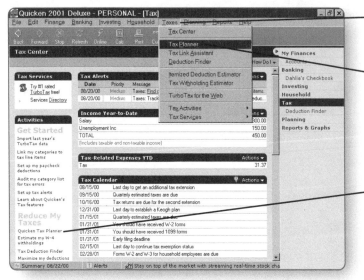

1. Click on **Taxes**. The Taxes menu will appear.

2. Click on **Tax Planner**. The Quicken Tax Planner will appear in the Tax Center.

NOTE

You can also find the Tax Planner by clicking on the Quicken Tax Planner link in the Tax Center.

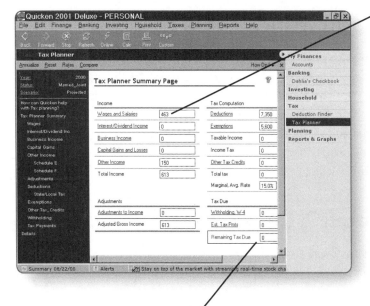

When the Tax Planner first opens, you should see the Tax Planner Summary Page. If you don't see this page, click on the Tax Planner Summary link found along the left side of the window. The Summary Page displays the totals from categories that are assigned to a tax form and line item in the appropriate income and deduction fields. This Tax Planner takes into account the information you entered in the Tax Profile.

NOTE

Look in the Tax Due section to see if you owe any taxes or might be due a refund.

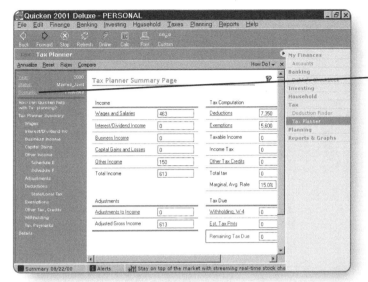

Forecasting Your Tax Liability

1. Click on the **Scenario link**. The Tax Planner Options page will appear.

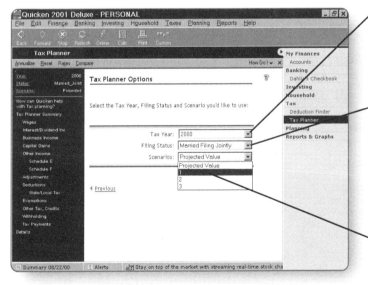

2. Click on the **Tax Year down arrow** and **select** the **tax year** for the projection. The year will appear in the text box.

3. Click on the **Filing Status down arrow** and **click** on the **tax filing status** that you want to use for the scenario from the drop-down list. The filing status will appear in the list box.

4. Click on the **Scenarios down arrow** and **click** on **1** to create your first tax scenario. The QTax dialog box will open.

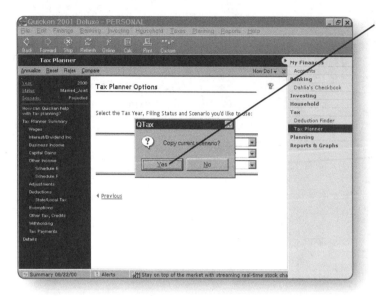

5. **Click** on **Yes** to use your actual Quicken information as the basis of the first scenario.

6. **Click** on the **Wages link**. The Wages page will appear.

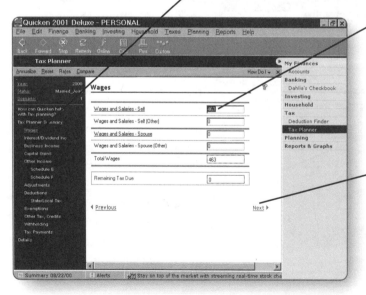

7. **Click** in the **text boxes** and **type** the **amounts** that you estimate will need to be declared on your tax return. As you move from field to field, notice that the amounts in the Tax Due section will change.

8. **Click** on the **Next link**. The Interest/Dividend Inc page will appear. Work your way through each page until you complete the information for the first scenario. When you have completed the first scenario, you can either create another scenario or compare the scenario with your actual information.

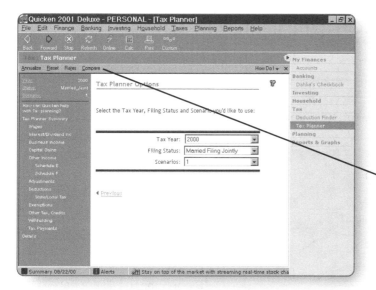

Comparing Tax Scenarios

Quicken offers a way for you to take closer look at the difference between your actual tax situation and any created scenarios.

1. Click on the **Compare button**. The Tax Scenario Comparisons dialog box will open.

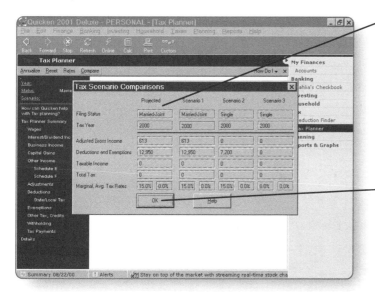

The Projected column shows your actual tax estimate based on the transactions you recorded in Quicken. The Scenario columns show the different scenarios that you created. Which scenario puts you at the best tax advantage?

2. Click on **OK**. The Tax Scenario Comparisons dialog box will close and you will return to the Quicken Tax Planner.

Compiling Tax Reports

The Tax Summary Report and the Tax Schedule Report can help you prepare your tax return. The Tax Summary Report lists each transaction that is assigned to a tax-related category and shows the totals for each category. The Tax Schedule Report lists each tax-related transaction according to the tax form and the line item in which it belongs.

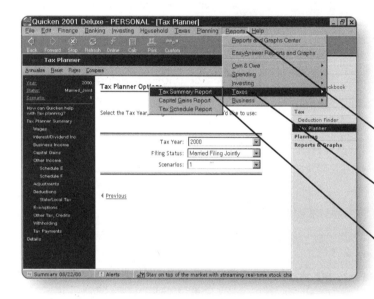

Creating a Tax Summary Report

1. Click on **Reports**. The Reports menu will appear.

2. Move the **mouse pointer** to Taxes. A submenu will appear.

3. Click on **Tax Summary Report**. The Tax Summary Report will appear in the Reports & Graphs window.

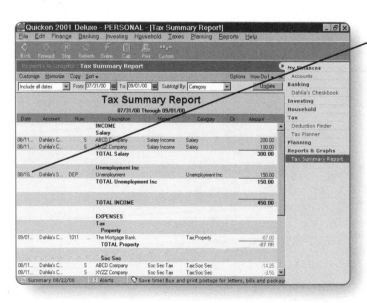

You'll find tax-related information from all of your accounts in the report. Tax-related transactions are grouped by category. There is a subtotal for each category.

Displaying the Tax Schedule Report

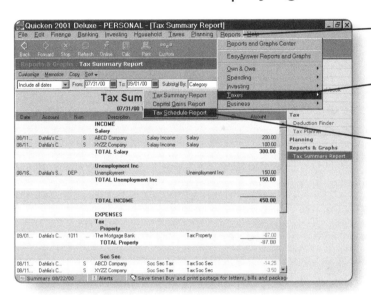

1. **Click** on **Reports**. The Reports menu will appear.

2. **Move** the **mouse pointer** to Taxes. A submenu will appear.

3. **Click** on **Tax Schedule Report**. The Tax Schedule Report will appear in the Reports & Graphs window.

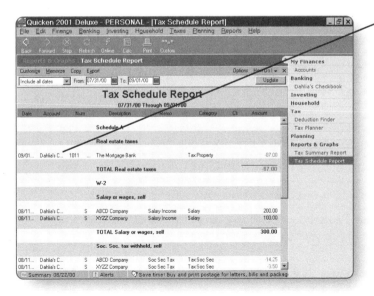

The Tax Schedule Report organizes your tax-related transactions by tax form and line item. Each line item is subtotaled.

Part III Review Questions

1. What is the easiest way to keep track of the cash you carry around in your pocket? *See "Creating a Petty Cash Account" in Chapter 9*

2. How do you keep track of cash that you've spent? *See "Recording Cash Purchases" in Chapter 9*

3. How do you set up your paycheck so that you do not have to record the income and taxes each time you are paid? *See "Setting Up Your Paycheck" in Chapter 10*

4. What type of account do you need to set up if you want to keep track of vacation time or sick leave that you have accrued? *See "Keeping Track of Vacation Time" in Chapter 10*

5. How do you keep track of the mortgage payments that you've made? *See "Setting Up a Mortgage Account" in Chapter 11*

6. If you have an adjustable rate mortgage, can Quicken keep track of the change in interest rates for you? *See "Setting Up a Mortgage Account" in Chapter 11*

7. How many different mortgage reports can you create and what purpose do they serve? *See "Producing Mortgage Reports" in Chapter 11*

8. Which Quicken tools can help you find tax deductions for which you qualify? *See "Finding Tax Deductions" in Chapter 12*

9. Is it possible to create forecasts that you can use to see what changes in income and expenses will do to your tax situation? *See "Estimating Taxes" in Chapter 12*

10. What reports can you produce to help you keep track of your tax situation? *See "Compiling Tax Reports" in Chapter 12*

Maintenence Tasks

13

Using the Quicken Tools

Quicken contains a number of tools that will make it easier for you to work with the program and to keep track of important financial and personal information. When you need to add up a few numbers quickly, open the calculator. If you want to see when your bills become due, whip out the calendar. To make it easier to address the envelopes in which you send your bill payments, keep creditor information in the address book. And, then, to make it easier to analyze your financial data, you can customize the various reports and graphs to display specific information. In this chapter, you'll learn how to:

- Get acquainted with the calculator
- Keep a calendar of important financial events
- Create an address book containing data on friends, family, and creditors
- Change the information displayed by reports and graphs

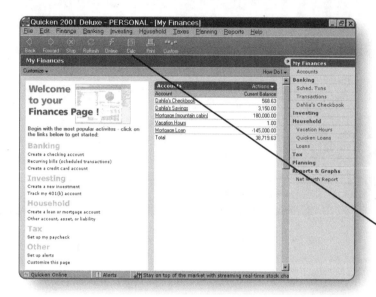

Working with the Calculator

No financial management program would be complete without a calculator. Whenever you need to add up a few numbers, use Quicken's handy calculator.

1. Click on the **Calc icon** on the Quicken toolbar located just below the menu bar. The Quicken Calculator will appear.

2. Click on the **number keys** that correspond with the first number in the calculation. The number will appear in the display area at the top of the calculator.

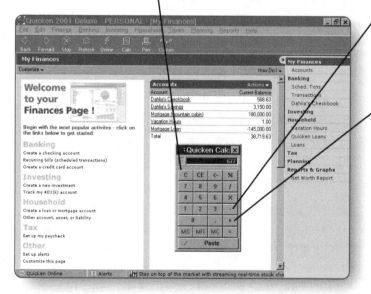

3a. Click on the **– key** if you want to subtract the next number from the first.

OR

3b. Click on the **+ key** if you want to add the next number to the first.

OR

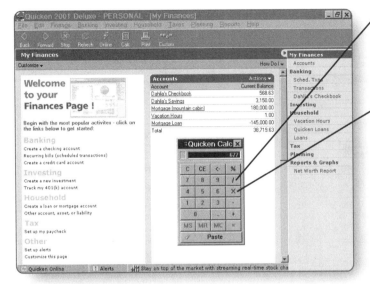

3c. **Click** on the **/ key** if you want to divide the first number by the next number.

OR

3d. **Click** on the **X key** if you want to multiply the first number by the next number.

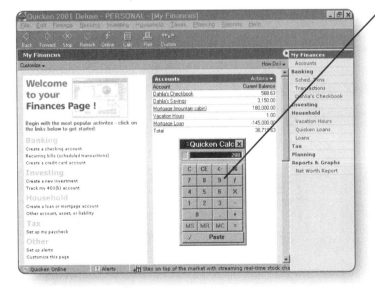

4. Click on the **number keys** that correspond with the next number in the calculation. The number will appear in the display area at the top of the calculator.

5. Add, subtract, multiply, or divide any **remaining numbers** in your calculation. The numbers will be computed in the calculation.

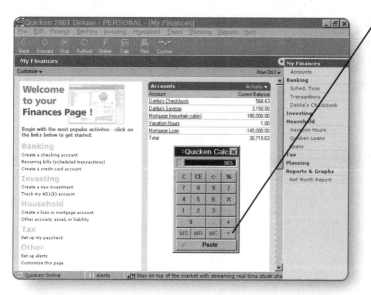

6. Click on the **= key**. The total for your calculation will appear in the calculator display.

NOTE

If the Num Lock key is active, you can also use the numeric keypad on your keyboard.

Here are a few tips to help you work with the calculator:

- If you want to clear the display to start a new calculation, click on the C key.

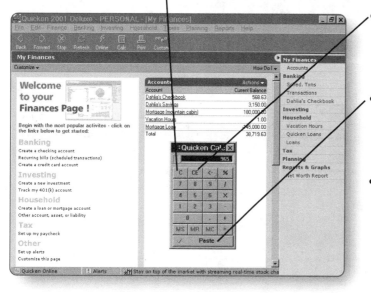

- If you notice you've entered the wrong number and you want to clear the number, click on the CE key.

- If you want to enter the number in the selected field of the register, click on the Paste button.

- Click on the Close button when you are finished with the calculator.

Staying on Track with the Calendar

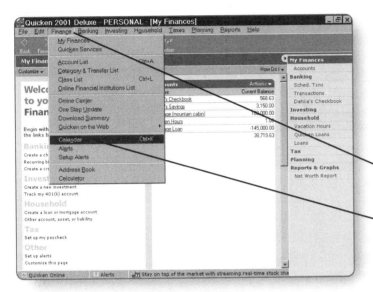

In Chapter 8, "Scheduling Payments," you learned how to tell Quicken to remind you when it was time to pay your bills. Another way to keep track of when payments are due is to open the Quicken Calendar.

1. Click on **Finance**. The Finance menu will appear.

2. Click on **Calendar**. The Financial Calendar will appear and the current date will be selected.

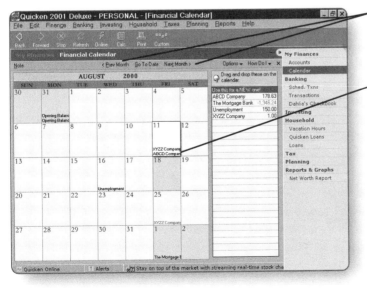

3. Click on the **Prev Month and Next Month buttons** to view different months.

4. Click on the **transaction information** for a selected date. The Transactions dialog box for the selected date will open.

5. **Click** on the **Edit button** if you need to make any changes to the transaction.

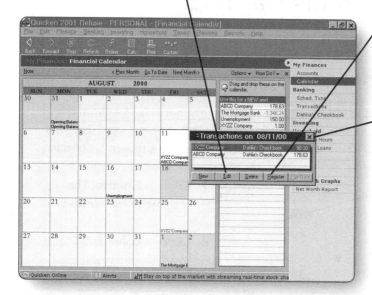

6. **Click** on the **Register button** if you want to view the account register in which the transaction was recorded.

7. **Click** on the **Close button** to close the Transactions dialog box.

NOTE

The red transaction information text indicates that a transaction is scheduled to be paid.

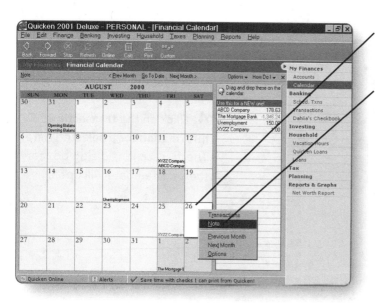

8. **Right-click** on a **date**. A menu will appear.

9. **Click** on **Note**. The Note dialog box will open.

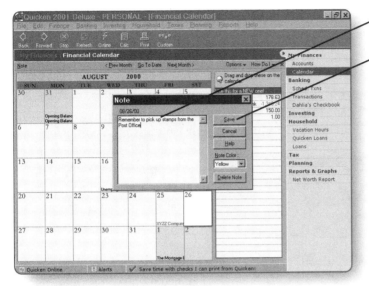

10. Type a **note** to yourself.

11. Click on **Save**. A note icon will appear in the corner of the selected date.

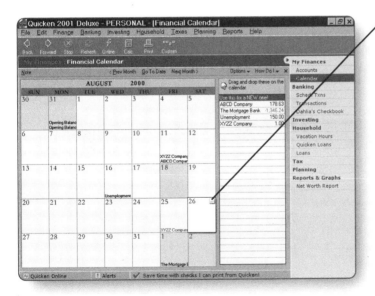

12. Click on the **note icon**. The Note dialog box will open and you can read, edit, or delete the note.

Storing Address Information

Some of your creditors may send a self-addressed envelope along with their bill. This makes it easier to pay your bills on time. For those creditors that do not provide this courtesy, you can store their address information in the Quicken address book. This address book isn't just for maintaining creditor information. You can also keep track of family and friends so that sending out the annual holiday letter isn't an envelope-addressing chore.

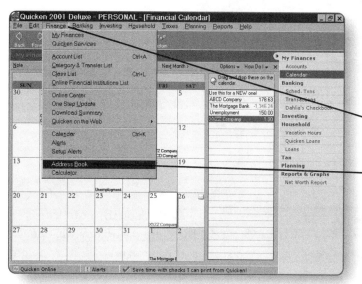

1. **Click** on **Finance**. The Finance menu will appear.

2. **Click** on **Address Book**. The Address Book will appear.

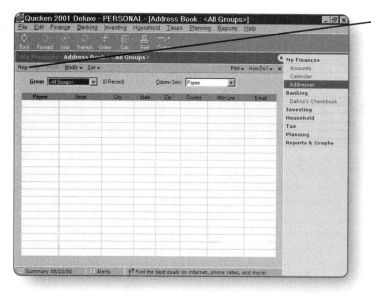

3. **Click** on **New**. The Edit Address Book Record dialog box will open.

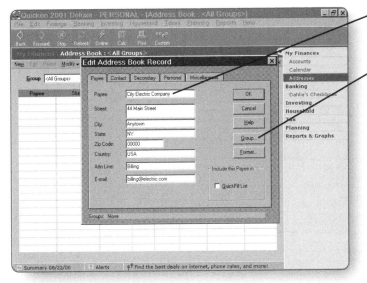

4. Click in a **text box** and **type** the requested **information**.

5. Click on the **Group button**. The Assign To Groups dialog box will open.

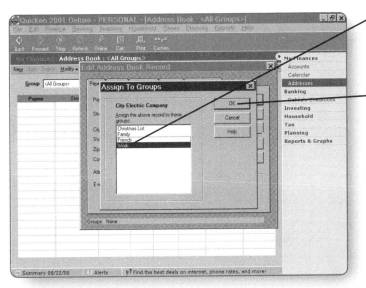

6. Click on the **group** to which you want to add the contact. The group will be selected.

7. Click on OK. The contact will be added to the group list and you will be returned to the Edit Address Book Record dialog box.

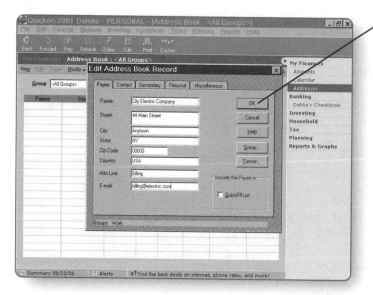

8. Click on **OK** when you have supplied all the information for the contact. The contact will be added to the address book list.

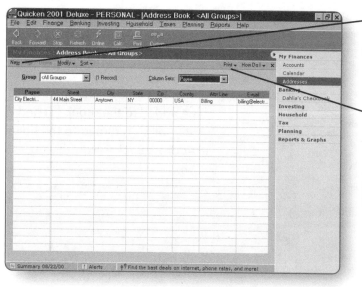

9. Add more **contacts** as needed.

NOTE

Click on the Print button to print the entire address book, or to print labels or an envelope for an individual contact.

Getting More from Graphs

As you work through this book and Quicken, you'll find that there are a number of reports and graphs that you can generate to see how well you are managing your finances. You can easily change the information that displays in these reports and graphs. Explore the Reports menu to get a feel for the types of graphs that are available. Or, open the Reports & Graphs Center by clicking on the Reports & Graphs QuickTab. You'll find graphs that show how much you spent during a specific time period, how your net worth has changed over time, and the difference between your budget and your actual spending.

Changing the Time Period Used by the Graph

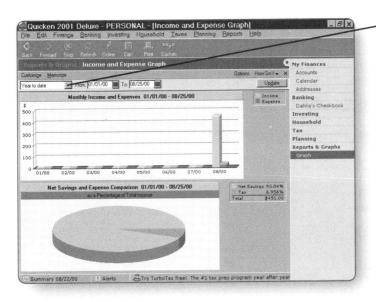

1. Click on the **Dates down arrow** and **click** on the **date range** that you want to show in the graph. The dates in the From and To text boxes will change. If you want to make changes to these dates, follow steps 2 and 3.

2. Click in the **From text box** and **type** the **beginning date** of the transactions you want to include in the graph.

3. Click in the **To text box** and **type** the **ending date** of the transactions that you want in the graph.

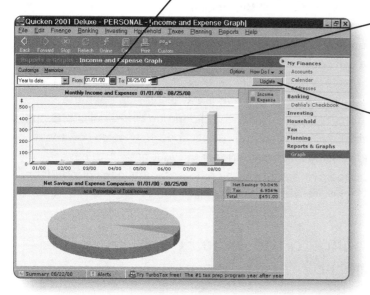

4. Click on the **Update button**. The information in the charts will be updated.

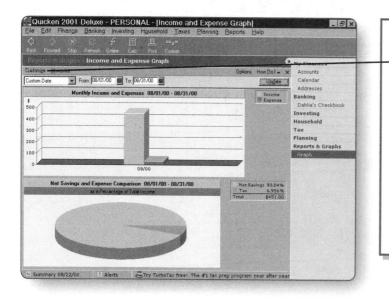

TIP

If you want to track your spending for a particular account or only certain categories, click on Customize. From the Customize Graph dialog box, clear the check boxes for those accounts and categories that you do not want to include in the chart.

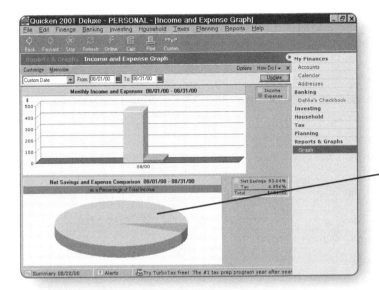

Zooming In on a Graph

If you want to see a section of a pie or bar chart in more detail, zoom in on that part of the graph.

1. Double-click on an **area** of the chart that you want to see in more detail. A QuickZoom Graph will appear.

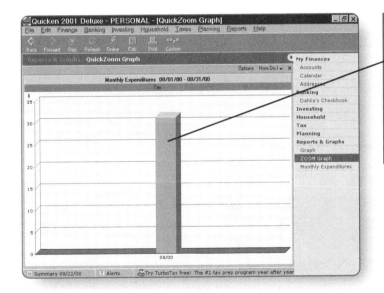

TIP

Double-click on an element in the chart to see a detailed list of the transactions included in the category for the selected time period.

Detailing Your Reports

After looking over a few reports, you may decide that they don't contain the information you need. You may want to change the range of dates used by the report, or you may not want to include all the categories. You can change anything you want. And, you can apply the changes to all reports that you create or just to an individual report.

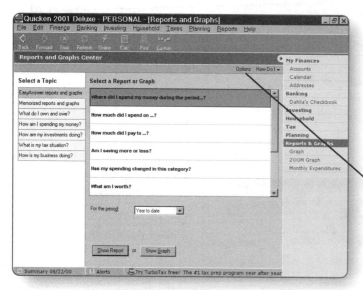

Changing the Default Report Options

To change the way information appears in all your future reports, you need to change the default report options.

1. Click on the **Options button**. You'll find this button on the main page of the Reports & Graphs Center and on every report and graph you create. The Report and Graph Options dialog box will open.

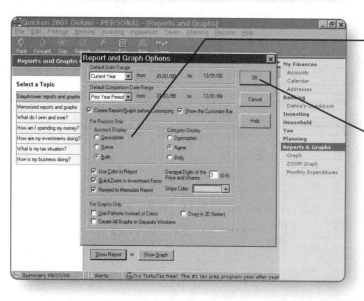

2. Click on those **options** that you want to change for future reports. The options will be selected.

3. Click on **OK**. The default options will be changed.

Customizing a Report

When you want to change the information in a single report, you'll need to customize that report. You can change the date range, the accounts used in the report, and the categories to be used. To begin, display the report that you want to change in the Reports & Graphs window.

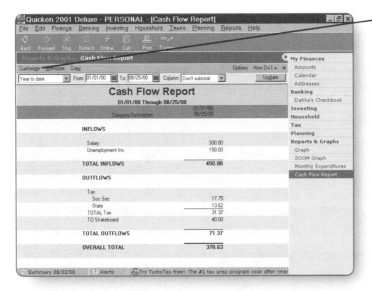

1. **Click** on **Customize**. The Customize Report dialog box will open and the Display tab should be on top.

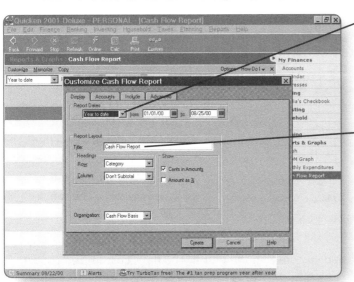

2. **Click** on the **Report Dates down arrow** and **click** on the **date range** that you want to use for the report. The date range will be selected.

3. **Click** in the **Title text box** and **type** a different **title** for the report.

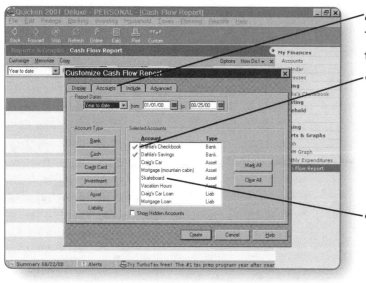

4. Click on the **Accounts tab**. The Accounts tab will move to the top of the stack.

- If an account is preceded by a check mark, the account will be included in the report. To remove the account from the report, click on the account and the check mark will disappear.

- If an account is preceded by a blank space, the account will not be included in the report. To include the account in the report, click on the account and a check mark will appear.

5. Click on the **Include tab**. The Include tab will move to the top of the stack.

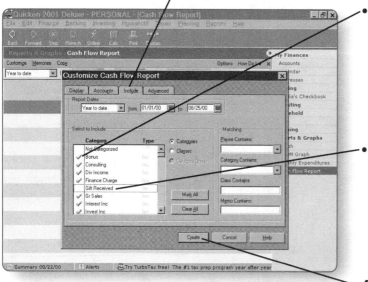

- If a category is preceded by a check mark, the category will be included in the report. To remove the category from the report, click on the category and the check mark will disappear.

- If a category is preceded by a blank space, the category will not be included in the report. To include the category in the report, click on the category and a check mark will appear.

6. Click on **Create** when you are finished customizing the graph. The new, customized report will appear in the Reports & Graphs window.

Saving Reports for Future Use

You may have created a custom report that you want to use over and over again. You'll want to memorize the report. There are several ways you can recall the report for future use.

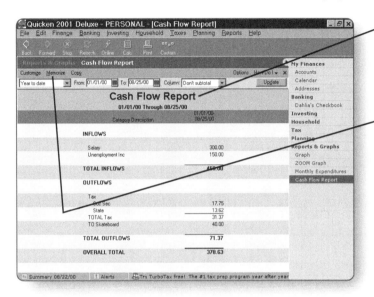

1. Display the **report** that you want to save for future use. The report will appear in the Reports & Graphs window.

2. Click on **Memorize**. The Memorize Report dialog box will open.

3. Click in the **Title text box** and **type** a **title** for the report.

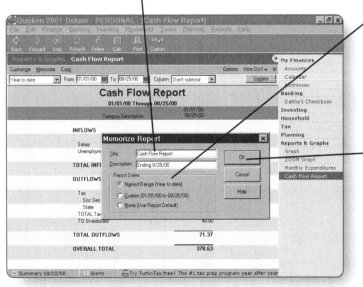

4. Click on an **option button** in the Report Dates section to select the dates that will be contained in the memorized report. The option will be selected.

5. Click on **OK**. The report will be memorized.

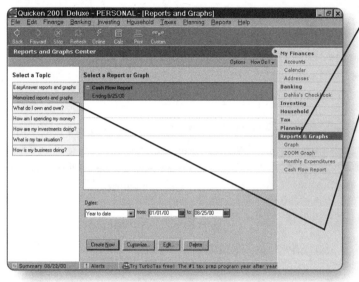

6. Click on the **Reports & Graphs QuickTab**. The Report and Graphs Center will appear.

7. Click on **Memorized reports and graphs**. You should see your memorized report in the list.

NOTE

You can also find the memorized report in the Reports menu. Open the Reports menu and move the mouse pointer to Memorized Reports and Graphs. A submenu will appear that contains all the reports that you've memorized.

14

Examining Your Spending Habits

Quicken contains many reports that you can use to quickly calculate where your money is going. By looking at your spending habits, you can see places where you can reduce your spending or better manage your money. This is a first step toward saving money and planning for major purchases, such as a car or home. After you've created a few reports, use the skills you learned in Chapter 13, "Using the Quicken Tools," to customize these reports to display specific information. In this chapter, you'll learn how to:

- Create some quick and snappy spending reports
- Take a look at where you've spent your hard-earned cash
- Create reports to help you better manage your money

Creating Quick Reports

When you want to quickly see how you are spending your money, turn to the EasyAnswer Reports and Graphs.

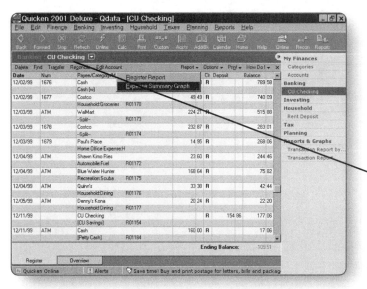

Graphing Your Spending

A simple pie chart is a quick way to graph your spending. You can create one that shows your top five spending categories.

1. Display the **account register** for which you want to view your spending. The register account window will appear.

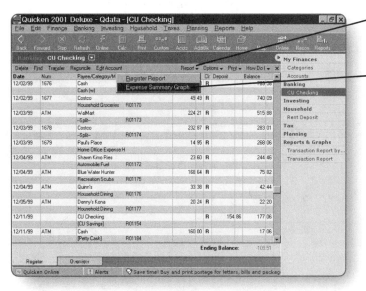

2. Click on **Report**. A menu will appear.

3. Click on **Expense Summary Graph**. The Expense Summary window will appear.

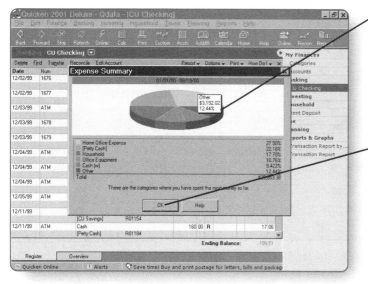

4. Hold the **mouse pointer** over an area of the pie chart. The name of the category, the dollar amount spent, and the percentage of total spending will appear in a ToolTip.

5. Click on **OK**. The Expense Summary window will close.

Using EasyAnswer Reports

If you'd like a little more information about your spending, but don't want to spend a lot of time looking for it, consult the EasyAnswer Reports.

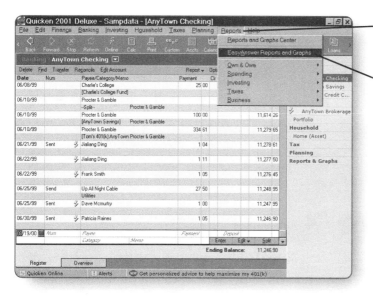

1. Click on **Reports**. The Reports menu will appear.

2. Click on **EasyAnswer Reports and Graphs**. The Reports and Graphs Center will appear.

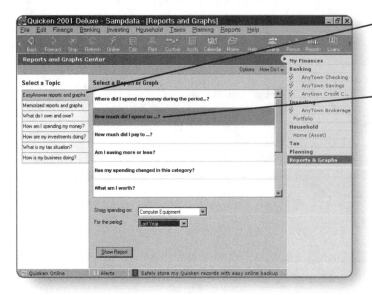

3. Click on the **EasyAnswer reports and graphs tab**. A list of questions will appear.

4. Click on a **question**. The question will be selected and the options shown below the list of questions will change depending on the question selected.

> **NOTE**
>
> The first five questions provide information about your spending habits.

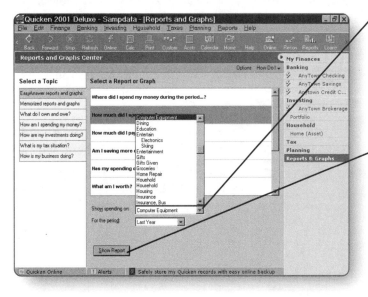

5. Click on the **down arrow** next to each list box and **click** on the **option** that will provide information to meet your needs. The option will appear in the list box.

6. Click on **Show Report**. The report will appear in the Reports & Graphs window.

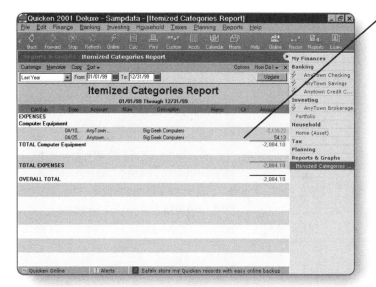

The report displays using the default options. You can further customize this and all other reports that you create. You learned how to do this in Chapter 13, "Using the Quicken Tools."

NOTE

To get back to the EasyAnswer Reports, click on the Reports & Graphs QuickTab.

Watching Your Cash Flow

Quicken provides a number of reports and graphs that show the sources of your income and how you spend it. These reports and graphs can help you keep track of your spending and aid you in building a budget and savings plan.

Creating an Account Balances Report

Before you look at your income sources and where you spent your money, you should find out the values of the checking, savings, mortgage, and other accounts that you set up in Quicken.

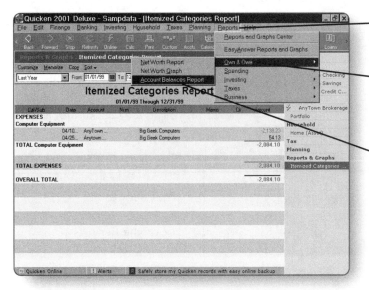

1. Click on **Reports**. The Reports menu will appear.

2. Move the **mouse pointer** to Own & Owe. A submenu will appear.

3. Click on **Account Balances Report**. The Account Balances Report will appear in the Reports & Graphs window.

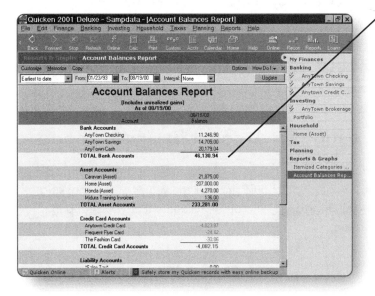

The Account Balances Report lists all accounts that you set up in the data file. The first accounts that are listed are your cash accounts, followed by personal assets, then your liabilities (such as credit cards and mortgages), and then your investments.

Producing an Income and Expense Graph

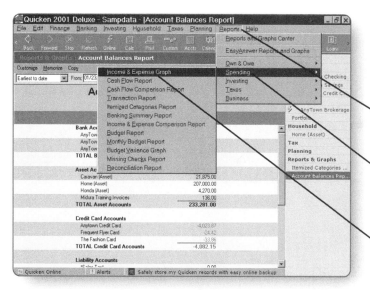

If you want a visual representation of your income and expenses, there's a quick graph that you can display.

1. **Click** on **Reports**. The Reports menu will appear.

2. **Move** the **mouse pointer** to Spending. A submenu will appear.

3. **Click** on **Income & Expense Graph**. The Income and Expense Graph will appear in the Reports & Graphs window.

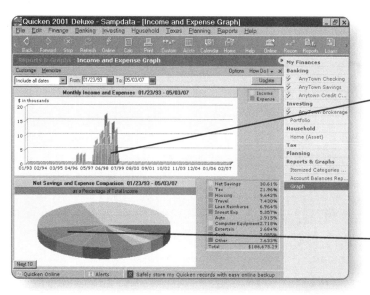

The Income and Expense Graph gives you two different views of your income and spending, as well as a helpful legend for each:

- **Bar chart**. This chart compares your monthly income and monthly expenses over time. Hold the mouse pointer over an element in the chart to display a ToolTip that describes the category and the dollar amount.

- **Pie chart.** This chart shows your total income divided into the amounts spent for each of your expenses. This chart only shows 10 categories. Click on the Next 10 button to see the rest of your category items.

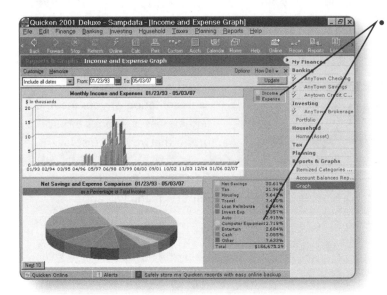

• **Legend**. The legend at the right of each chart shows the colors that represent categories. You'll find other information about the categories in the legend.

Creating a Cash Flow Report

Now that you've seen a few overview pictures of your spending, it's time to create a Cash Flow Report. A Cash Flow Report shows your money coming in and going out.

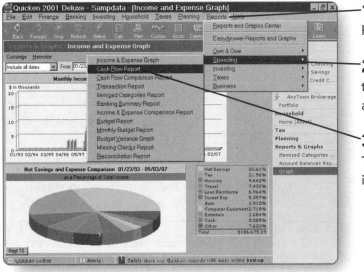

1. Click on **Reports**. The Reports menu will appear.

2. Move the **mouse pointer** to Spending. A submenu will appear.

3. Click on **Cash Flow Report**. The Cash Flow Report will appear in the Reports & Graphs window.

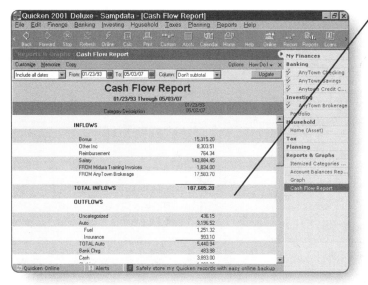

At the bottom of the Cash Flow Report, you'll see how much money you should have been able to save during the time period covered by the report.

Building a Cash Flow Comparison Report

Create a Comparison Report if you want to see how your spending compares for different time periods (for example, this year and last year, or this month and last month).

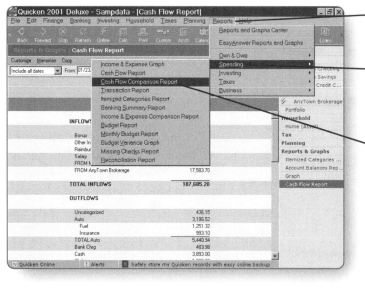

1. Click on **Reports**. The Reports menu will appear.

2. Move the **mouse pointer** to Spending. A submenu will appear.

3. Click on **Cash Flow Comparison Report**. The Comparison Report will appear in the Reports & Graphs window.

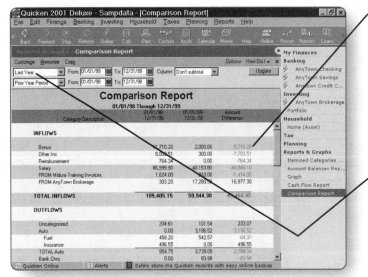

By default, the Comparison Report lists the cash flow summary for each year that is contained in your Quicken data file.

TIP

You can change the periods that are used for comparison by selecting date options from the drop-down lists.

Itemizing Spending Categories

A Cash Flow Report can also provide details of each transaction in the income and expense categories.

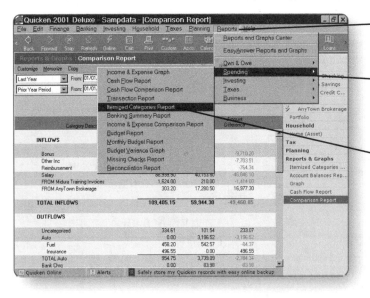

1. Click on **Reports**. The Reports menu will appear.

2. Move the **mouse pointer** to Spending. A submenu will appear.

3. Click on **Itemized Categories Report**. The Itemized Categories Report will appear in the Reports & Graphs window.

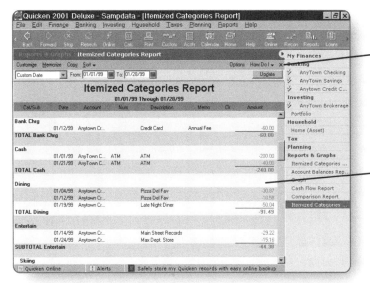

NOTE

If you won't be using a report again, click on the Close button in the report's window.

The Itemized Categories Report lists each of the categories that have been set up in Quicken and each transaction that was posted to a category. There is also a subtotal showing the amount spent in a category.

15

Preserving Your Financial Records

The importance of protecting your financial records cannot be stressed enough. You can apply passwords to data files to keep your financial data out of the view of prying eyes and prevent the unauthorized changing of financial transactions. Be sure to keep backups of data files—it only takes a few seconds. It could take months to recreate the data from scratch. In this chapter, you'll learn how to:

- Password protect data files and transaction records
- Back up and restore data files

Assigning Passwords

Passwords are a great way to keep your financial records private. You can also prevent anyone from making changes to transactions without your authorization.

Protecting Transactions with Passwords

When you assign a password to a transaction or to a group of transactions, you're only preventing others from making changes to transactions within a specified time period. Other people will still be able to view the account registers and other Quicken features. Once you have password protected the transactions, you can change the password by following the same steps.

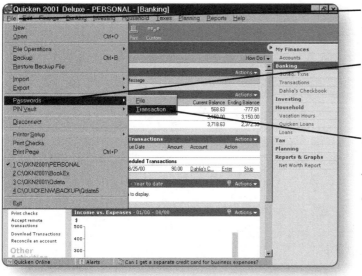

1. Click on **File**. The File menu will appear.

2. Move the **mouse pointer** to Passwords. A second menu will appear.

3. Click on **Transaction**. The Password to Modify Existing Transactions dialog box will open.

4. Type a **password** in the Password text box. Asterisks will appear in place of the characters you typed. Make sure you keep your password stored in a safe place.

5. Type the same **password** in the Confirm Password text box. Asterisks will appear in the text box.

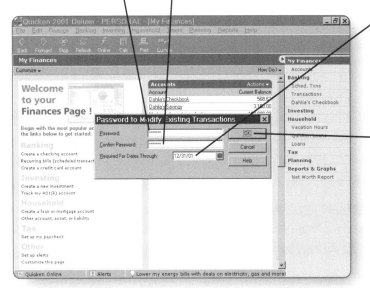

6. Type the **date** of the last transaction that you want password protected in the Required For Dates Through text box.

7. Click on **OK**. The transactions from the date you opened the data file until the last transaction date you specified will be password protected. Any attempt to edit these transactions will open a password dialog box, at which time a password is needed to continue.

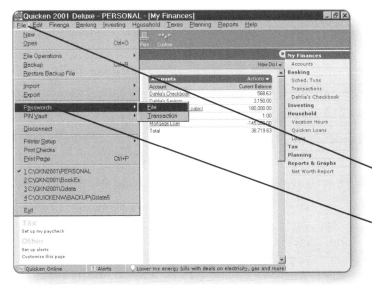

Restricting Access to a File

If you want to prevent others from seeing your account registers and other account information, use a file password.

1. Click on **File**. The File menu will appear.

2. Move the **mouse pointer** to Passwords. A submenu will appear.

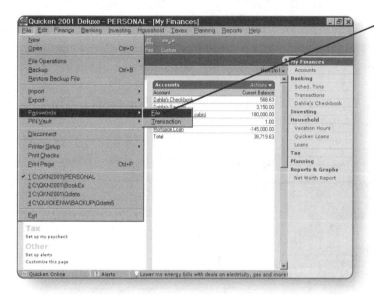

3. Click on **File**. The Set Up Password dialog box will open.

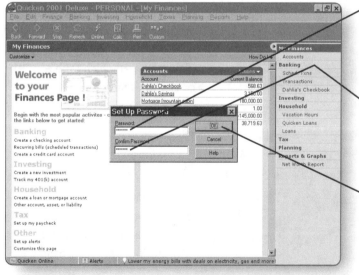

4. Type a **password** in the Password text box. Asterisks will appear in place of the characters you typed.

5. Type the same **password** in the Confirm Password text box. Asterisks will appear in the text box.

6. Click on **OK**. The file will be password protected. Whenever this data file is opened, a password will be required.

TIP

You can change your password later. Open the File menu, select Passwords, and then File. Make the changes in the dialog box that opens.

Keeping Backup Files

It's always a good idea to back up your Quicken data file after you enter any transactions or perform any other actions in Quicken. That way you'll always have a safe copy of your most recent financial records.

Creating a Backup File

The processes of backing up and restoring a Quicken data file are the same, whether you are restoring the data file to the same computer or to a different computer.

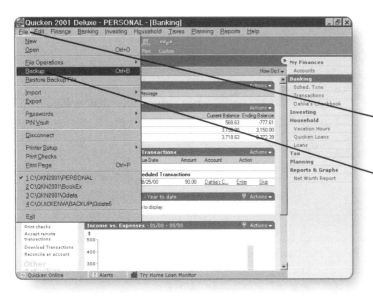

1. Open the Quicken **data file** that you want to back up. The data file will appear in the Quicken window.

2. Click on **File**. The File menu will appear.

3. Click on **Backup**. The Quicken Backup dialog box will open.

> **NOTE**
>
> Make sure that you have a blank, formatted backup media (such as a floppy disk, a tape backup, or a CD-ROM) in the drive to which you will copy the backup data file.

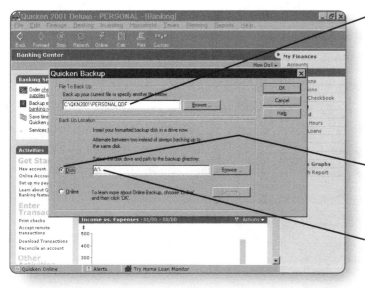

4. Verify that the **file** to be backed up is the one listed in the Back up your current file or specify another file below text box. If it isn't the right file, use the Browse button to select the file that you want to back up.

5. Click on the **Disk option button**. The option will be selected.

6. Type the **drive and path** where the backup file will be stored in the Disk text box.

7. Place the **backup disk** in the appropriate disk drive.

8. Click on **OK**. The information will be backed up to the drive you specified. When the backup is complete, a confirmation dialog box will open.

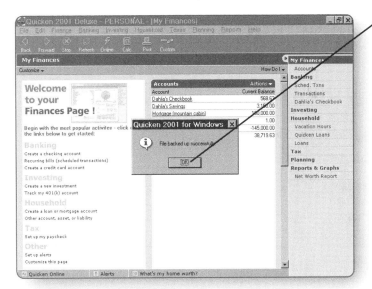

9. Click on **OK**. The data file will be backed up and you can remove the backup media from the drive.

Restoring a Backup File

You can restore your Quicken data file to a different computer than the one on which you normally store your Quicken files.

1. Open Quicken on the computer to which you are going to copy the file. The Quicken window will appear.

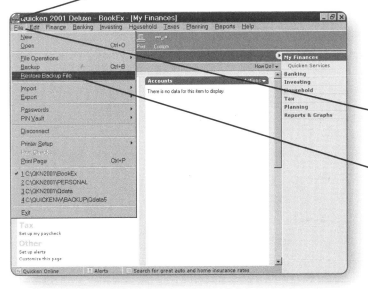

2. Place the **disk** that contains the backup file in the appropriate drive. This is the backup disk that you created in the last section.

3. Click on **File**. The File menu will appear.

4. Click on **Restore Backup File**. The Select Restore Drive dialog box will open.

5. Click on the **Restore files from Drive down arrow** and **click** on the **drive** where you placed the backup disk. The drive letter will appear in the list box.

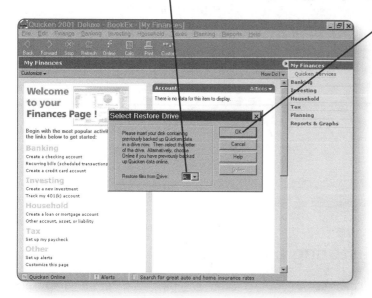

6. Click on **OK**. The Restore Quicken File dialog box will open.

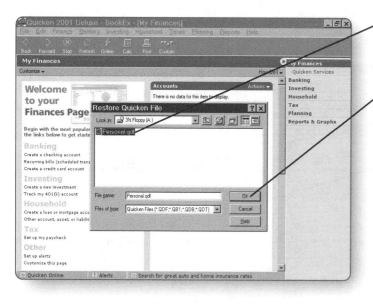

7. Click on the **data file** that you want to restore. The file will be selected.

8. Click on **OK**. A confirmation dialog box will open.

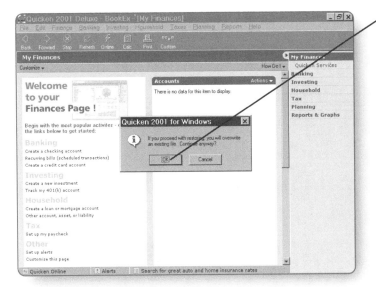

9. **Click** on **OK**. The data file will be restored on your computer and a confirmation dialog box will open.

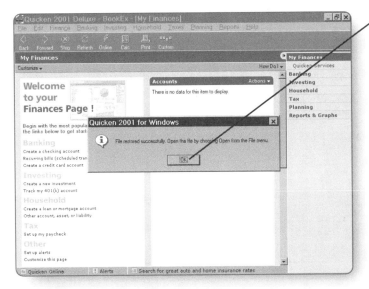

10. **Click** on **OK**. You can now open the restored file by choosing Open from the File menu.

16

Preparing for a New Year

Before you close out your books for the old year, take some time and run a few reports. These reports can show you how well you managed your finances for the past year. Just as it is important to keep a backup of your Quicken data file, it's also a good idea to keep a paper copy of your financial picture. You'll then need to do some file maintenance to your data file so that Quicken can start the new year on the right foot. You'll want to create a separate archive of the past year's financial records. And, you'll want to store this in a safe place, away from fire and theft. In this chapter, you'll learn how to:

- Create year-end financial reports
- Archive a year-end data file
- Prepare a data file for the new year

Producing Year-End Reports

You can produce several reports to take a look at your financial picture for the past year. It's a good idea to print a copy of these reports so that you can file them away with your tax returns and other important financial information.

Creating a Summary Report

The Summary Report shows you the totals of your income and expenses. Your income and expenses are broken into categories showing the total recorded in each category. It does not list the individual transactions in the category. You can either display an annual total for each category, or you can break up the categories into time periods, such as months or quarters.

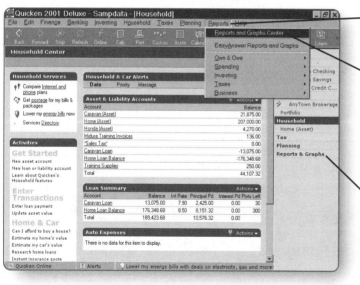

1. **Click** on **Reports**. The Reports menu will appear.

2. **Click** on **Reports and Graphs Center**. The Reports and Graphs Center window will appear.

NOTE

You can also click on the Reports & Graphs QuickTab, if it is available.

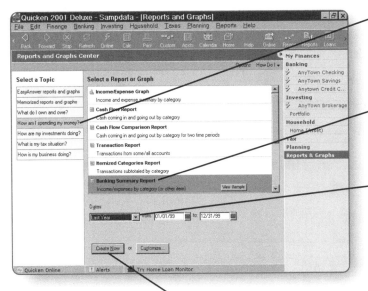

3. **Click** on the **How am I spending my money? tab**. The list of reports that will answer that question will appear.

4. **Click** on **Banking Summary Report**. The report will be selected.

5. **Click** on the **Dates down arrow** and **click** on the **desired date** from the drop-down list. The date you select will appear in the list box.

6. **Click** on the **Create Now button**. The Summary Report will appear.

TIP

Click on the View Sample button if you want to see a miniature example of the report.

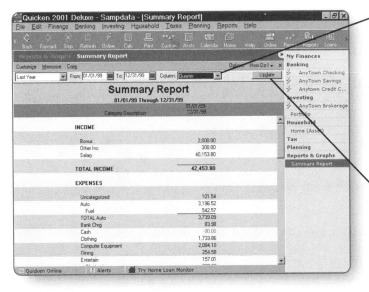

7. **Click** on the **Column down arrow** and **click** on a **time period** if you want the information in the report to be broken into time periods and then totaled for the entire year. The time period will appear in the list box.

8. **Click** on the **Update button**. The report will be updated.

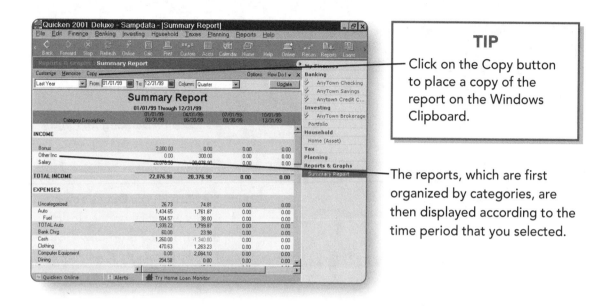

TIP

Click on the Copy button to place a copy of the report on the Windows Clipboard.

The reports, which are first organized by categories, are then displayed according to the time period that you selected.

Determining Your Net Worth

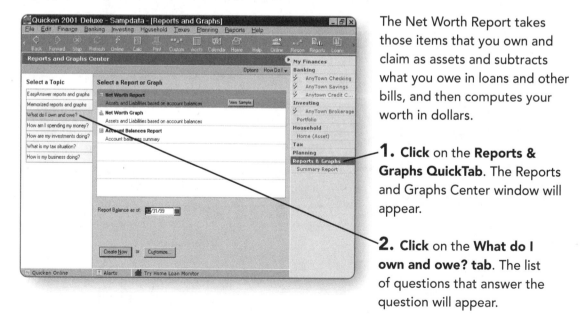

The Net Worth Report takes those items that you own and claim as assets and subtracts what you owe in loans and other bills, and then computes your worth in dollars.

1. Click on the **Reports & Graphs QuickTab**. The Reports and Graphs Center window will appear.

2. Click on the **What do I own and owe? tab**. The list of questions that answer the question will appear.

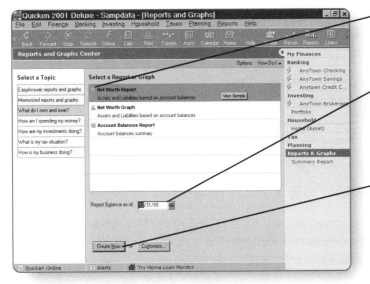

3. **Click** on **Net Worth Report**. The Net Worth Report will be selected.

4. **Click** in the **Report Balance as of text box** and **type** the **date** of the last day of the previous year.

5. **Click** on the **Create Now button**. The Net Worth Report will appear in the Reports & Graphs window.

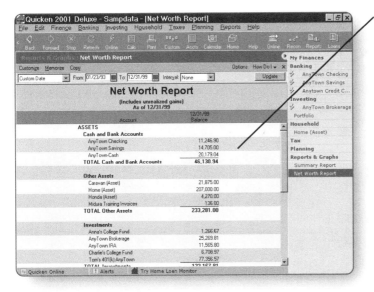

In bookkeeping terms, the Net Worth Report is the same as a balance sheet. You'll first see each of your assets listed with a total for the entire list of assets. You'll then see all your liabilities (or debts and loans) with their respective amounts. At the bottom of the report, you'll find your net worth.

Performing Year-End File Maintenance

Quicken offers two methods to close out your data file at the end of the year. It is recommended that you use the archival method unless your Quicken data file has become quite large. If it has, create a new file.

Archiving Your Files

When you archive data files, you copy the previous year's transactions to a separate file. You can then keep this file in a safe place. By doing this, you keep the previous year's transactions in the file you use for the current year. The advantage to this is that you can use the previous year's information when you run reports and create budgets and forecasts. The disadvantage is that your Quicken data file may become large and difficult to back up.

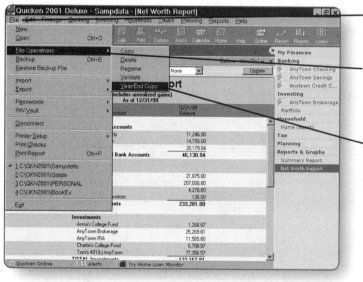

1. Click on **File**. The File menu will appear.

2. Move the **mouse pointer** to File Operations. A submenu will appear.

3. Click on **Year-End Copy**. The Year-End Copy dialog box will open.

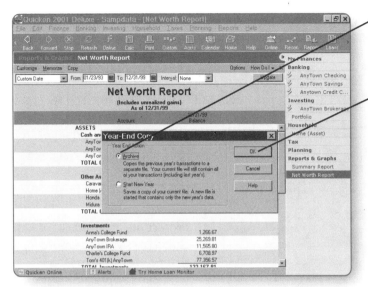

4. **Click** on the **Archive option button**, if it is not already selected.

5. **Click** on **OK**. The Archive File dialog box will open.

6. **Click** in the **Archive Old Data to File text box** and **type** a **file name** for the file that will contain the past year's transactions. You could also use the default file name.

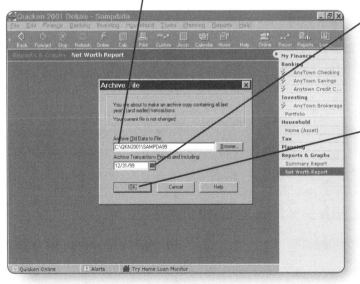

7. **Click** in the **Archive Transactions Prior to and Including text box** and **type** the **ending date** of the transactions that you want to archive.

8. **Click** on **OK**. The archive process will start and the File Copied Successfully dialog box will open when the process has finished.

9. **Click** on the **Current file option button**, if it is not already selected. The option will be selected.

10. **Click** on **OK**. The original data file will appear in the Quicken window and all of your transactions for the prior year will still appear in the registers.

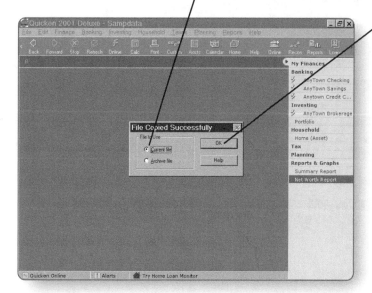

TIP

Protect the archived file with a password to ensure that no changes are made to it. See Chapter 15, "Preserving Your Financial Records," if you need help.

Setting Up a New File

By setting up a new file in which to keep your financial records for the new year, you only keep those transactions that are not reconciled in the previous year. The advantage is a smaller file size. The disadvantage is that you will not be able to compare your income and spending from previous years to the current year.

1. **Click** on **File**. The File menu will appear.

2. **Move** the **mouse pointer** to File Operations. A submenu will appear.

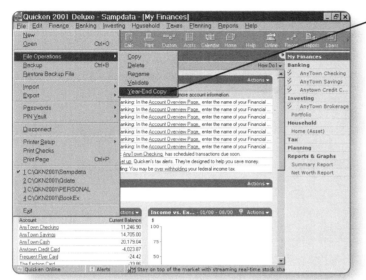

3. **Click** on **Year-End Copy**. The Year-End Copy dialog box will open.

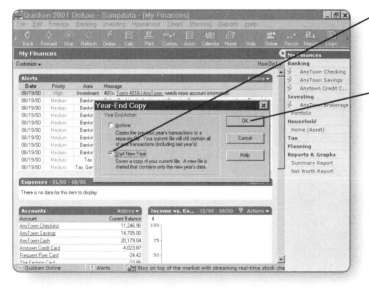

4. **Click** on the **Start New Year option button**. The option will be selected.

5. **Click** on **OK**. The Start New Year dialog box will open.

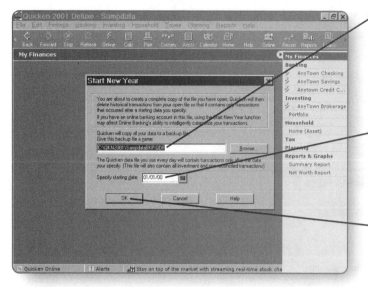

6. **Click** in the **Give this backup file a name text box** and **type** a **file name** for the file into which you want to place all the prior year's transactions.

7. **Click** in the **Specify starting date field** and **type** the **date** on which the new file will commence.

8. **Click** on **OK**. The transactions for the prior year will be archived and the File Copied Successfully dialog box will open.

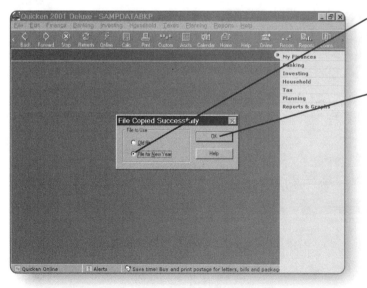

9. **Click** on the **File for New Year option button**, if it is not already selected.

10. **Click** on **OK**. You will return to the Quicken window.

Part IV Review Questions

1. When you need to perform a few math calculations, where should you go? *See "Working with the Calculator" in Chapter 13*

2. Where can you keep track of contact information for family, friends, and creditors? *See "Staying on Track with the Calendar" in Chapter 13*

3. How do you change the date range that is used to generate reports? *See "Detailing Your Reports" in Chapter 13*

4. What is the fastest way to see where you've spent your money? *See "Creating Quick Reports" in Chapter 14*

5. Which reports can you create if you want to see where your money comes from and how it is spent? *See "Watching Your Cash Flow" in Chapter 14*

6. If you don't want others to see your Quicken data, how can you prevent access to your data? *See "Assigning Passwords" in Chapter 15*

7. How do you back up your Quicken data file? *See "Keeping Backup Files" in Chapter 15*

8. What reports should you produce at the end of each year? *See "Producing Year-End Reports" in Chapter 16*

9. How do you store data for a previous year while still being able to use the information during the current year? *See "Archiving Your Files" in Chapter 16*

10. How do you start a completely new file for each year's financial information? *See "Setting Up a New File" in Chapter 16*

PART V

Learn to Spend Wisely

17

Budgeting and Your Finances

If you feel that you need to get a handle on your spending habits, your first step is to create a budget, which can help you limit what you spend on various items. Quicken contains an easy-to-use feature that helps you create and maintain a budget. You can elect to start your budget from scratch, or you can use data from transactions you've already entered into Quicken. After you get some preliminary figures entered, you can adjust the numbers so that you are spending the desired amount. After you put together a budget, you'll need to monitor your progress; Quicken can help warn you when you're getting dangerously close to going over budget. In this chapter, you'll learn how to:

- Create a fast and easy budget to fit your needs
- Warn yourself before you exceed budget goals
- Watch your progress toward meeting budget goals

Building a Budget

Your first step in building a budget is to add some preliminary numbers to the budget and determine which categories you want to track.

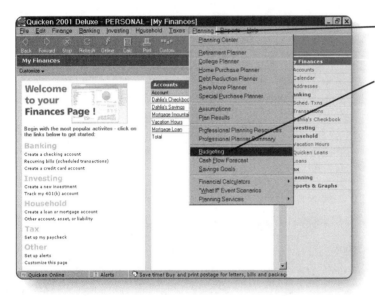

1. Click on **Planning**. The Planning menu will appear.

2. Click on **Budgeting**. The First Time in Budgets dialog box will open.

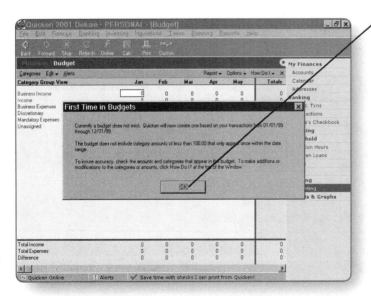

3. Click on **OK**. The Budget will appear in the Planning window. The budget numbers that appear may or may not be the numbers with which you want to start.

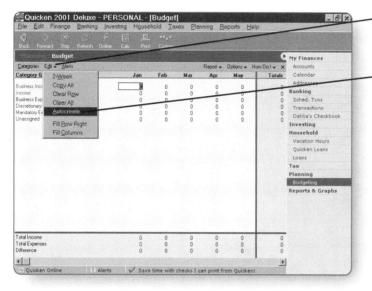

4. Click on **Edit**. A menu will appear.

5. Click on **Autocreate**. The Automatically Create Budget dialog box will open.

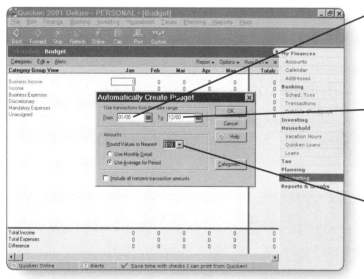

6. Click in the **From text box** and **type** the **beginning date** of the transactions that you want to include in the budget.

7. Click in the **To text box** and **type** the **ending date** of the transactions that you want to include in the budget.

8. Click on the **Round Values to Nearest down arrow** and **click** on the **value** to which you want numbers rounded. The value will appear in the list box.

9a. Click on the **Use Monthly Detail option button** if you want to use your actual monthly expenditures in the budget. The option will be selected.

OR

9b. Click on the **Use Average for Period option button** if you want to average expenditures for the period you selected and distribute them evenly among budget periods. The option will be selected.

10. Click on **OK**. You will return to the budget.

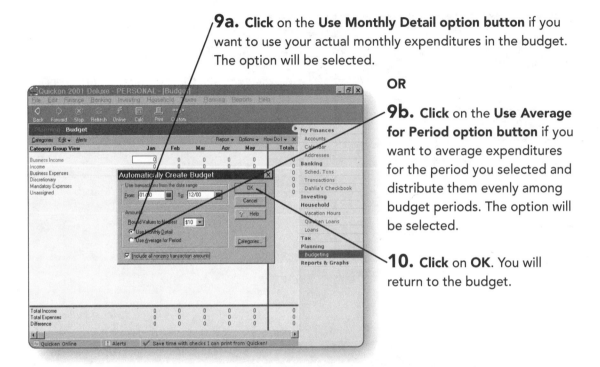

Adding and Removing Categories in the Budget List

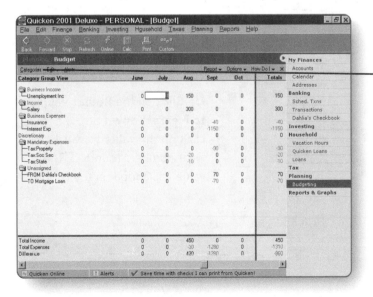

You can change the categories that appear in the budget.

1. Click on **Categories**. The Select Categories to Include dialog box will open.

2. Click on a **category** that has a check mark to the left of the category name. The check mark will be cleared and the category will not be included in the budget.

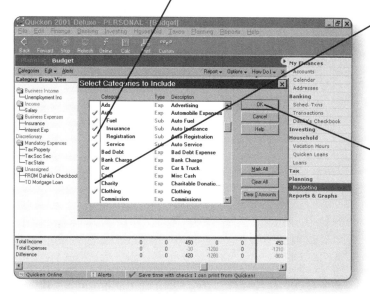

3. Click on a **category** that has a blank space to the left of the category name. A check mark will appear in the space and the category will be included in the budget.

4. Click on **OK**. The budget will be updated and will show only those categories that you've selected. Now you're ready to begin adjusting the budget numbers.

Editing Budget Amounts

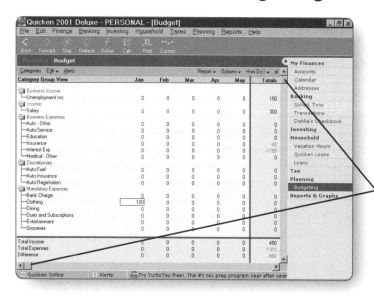

Your budget now contains only those categories that you selected along with some starting budget numbers, which are based on a selected period of past transactions. You can further adjust these numbers, if needed.

1. Click and drag the **scroll bars** to display the category and month for which you want to change a budget amount. A different area of the Budget window will appear.

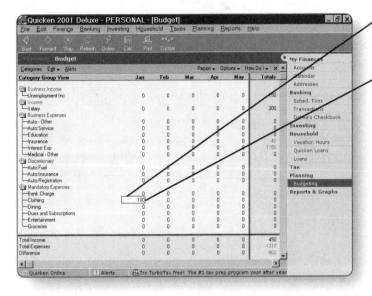

2. Click on an **amount field**. The amount will be selected.

3. Type a **new amount** and **press** the **Enter key**.

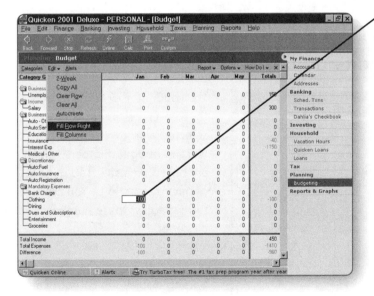

4. Click on the **amount field** that contains the value that you want to use to fill the amount fields located to the right (and on the same row). The field will be selected.

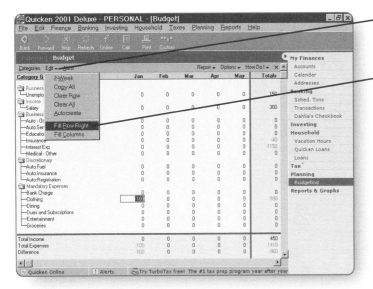

5. Click on **Edit**. A menu will appear.

6. Click on **Fill Row Right**. A confirmation dialog box will open.

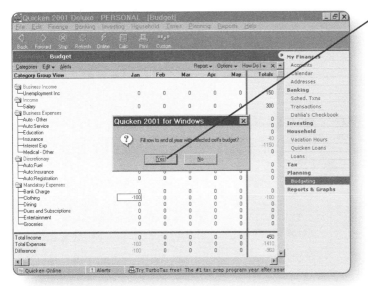

7. Click on **Yes**. The selected amount will be copied to all of the fields to the right of the selected field.

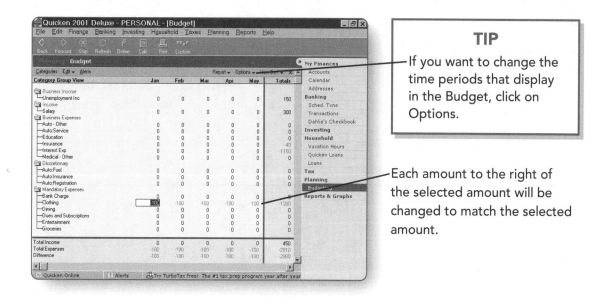

TIP

If you want to change the time periods that display in the Budget, click on Options.

Each amount to the right of the selected amount will be changed to match the selected amount.

Setting Budget Alerts

Quicken can tell you when you are close to your category spending limit. You need to set monthly limits for each category and decide how far in advance you'd like to be warned.

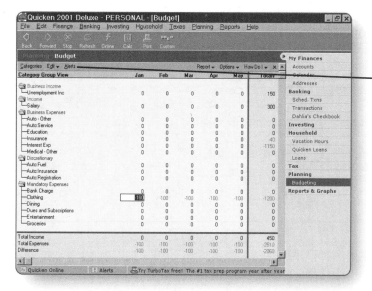

Determining Spending Limits

1. Click on **Alerts**. The Set Up Alerts dialog box will open. You'll also notice that the Banking tab is at the top of the stack and that the Monthly Expenses account alert is selected. This is the alert for your budget items.

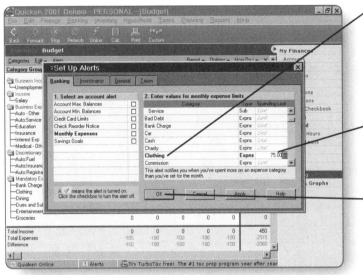

2. **Click** on the **Category field** for each budget item for which you want to set an alarm. The cursor will appear in the Spending Limit field.

3. **Type** the **amount** that you want to set as the spending limit for the month.

4. **Click** on **OK** when you finish setting spending limits for the categories. The alert will be set.

Setting Global Alert Options

If you don't want to set a limit for each individual budget item, you can set alerts based on the amount of the budget item. These alerts are set for all categories in your budget.

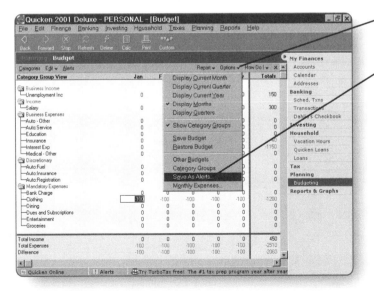

1. **Click** on **Options**. A menu will appear.

2. **Click** on **Save As Alerts**. The Save Budget Alerts Options dialog box will open.

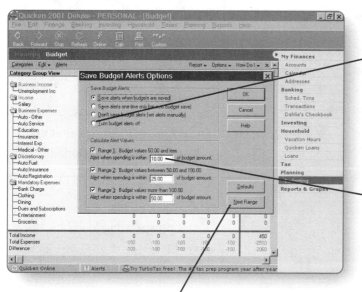

NOTE

If you do not want to be notified when you are approaching a spending limit, click on the Turn budget alerts off option button.

3. **Click** in a **Calculate Alert Values text box** and **type** the **dollar amount** at which you want to be warned that you are reaching a spending limit.

4. **Click** on **Next Range**. The Calculate Alert Values section will change to show a different range of budget values.

5. **Repeat steps 3 and 4** until you finish setting spending limits.

6. **Click** on **OK**. You will return to the Budget window. When you approach a spending limit, Quicken will let you know.

Staying on Budget

Once you have your budget in place, you can run a number of reports that will help you determine just how well you are keeping to your budget goals.

Creating a Budget Report

The Budget Report lists each category you are tracking in your budget. The report shows your actual spending to date compared to the amount you budgeted for the year for each category item.

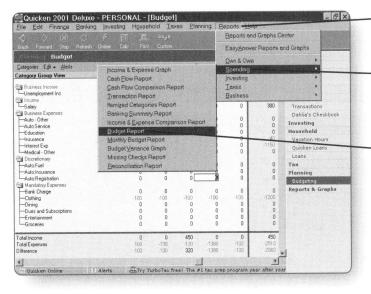

1. Click on **Reports**. The Reports menu will appear.

2. **Move** the **mouse pointer** to Spending. A submenu will appear.

3. Click on **Budget Report**. The Budget Report will appear in the Reports & Graphs window.

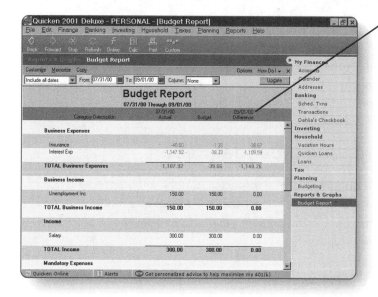

The last column in the Budget Report tells you how close you are to actually meeting your budget.

- **Positive number.** A positive number means that you are spending less than you budgeted.

- **Negative number.** A negative number means that you are spending over your budget limit.

Displaying the Monthly Budget Report

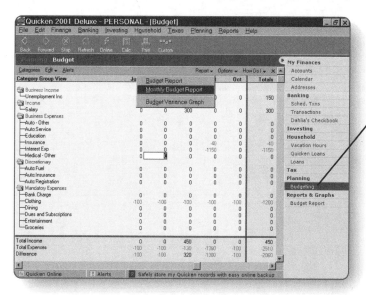

If you want to see your budget information broken down into months, you can use the Monthly Budget Report.

1. Click on the **Budgeting QuickTab**. The Budget will appear in the Planning window.

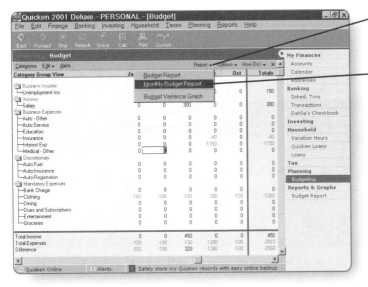

2. Click on **Report**. A menu will appear.

3. Click on **Monthly Budget Report**. The Monthly Budget Report will appear in the Reports & Graphs window.

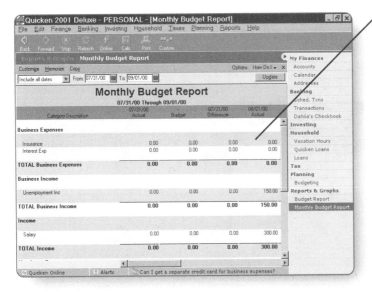

The Monthly Budget Report gives you the same information as the Budget Report, but the information is broken into months.

Producing a Budget Variance Graph

If you want a visual representation of how well you are meeting your budget goals, try out the Budget Variance Graph.

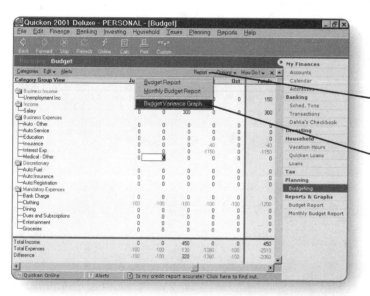

1. Click on the **Budgeting QuickTab**. The Budget will appear in the Planning window.

2. Click on **Report**. A menu will appear.

3. Click on **Budget Variance Graph**. The Budget Variance Graph will appear in the Reports & Graphs window.

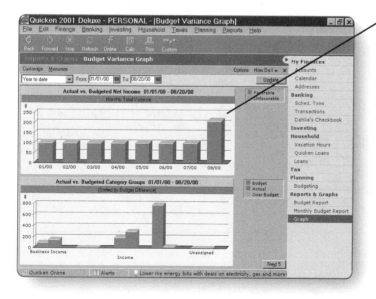

The graph shows how well you are meeting your budget in terms of income and category groups.

18

Creating a Savings Plan

Having money stashed away in a savings account is always a good idea, no matter what the reason. You may want to keep a reserve in case your regular source of income disappears. You may also want to save money to buy a particular item, such as a computer or a musical instrument, instead of taking out a loan or using your credit card. In this instance, you need to know what the item will cost and then set up a schedule to make regular savings contributions. Quicken provides lots of savings ideas and can help you save for a rainy day. In this chapter, you'll learn how to:

- Find resources that can help you build a savings plan
- Set aside money for special purchases
- Create savings goals and contribute to them

Learning to Save

Quicken contains a handy tool that walks you through the process of determining where you can cut money from your expenses and begin saving. The Save More Planner can also show you other places where you can learn more about saving money, and how to use Quicken to help you in this process.

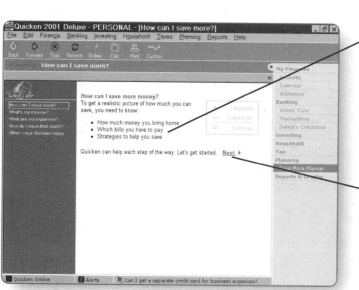

1. Click on **Planning**. The Planning menu will appear.

2. Click on **Save More Planner**. The Save More Planner will appear in the Planning window.

NOTE
You can also click on the How can I save more money? link in the Planning Center.

3. Read the **instructions**. The Save More Planner will walk you through the process of finding ways to save more money. Make sure you read each screen carefully as you work with the planner.

4. Click on **Next**. The What's my monthly income? screen will appear.

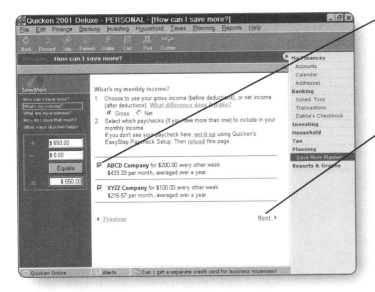

5. **Click** in the **check box** next to the paycheck that you want to include in your savings calculation. A check mark will appear in the check box.

6. **Click** on **Next**. The What are my expenses? screen will appear. This screen uses either the amounts you entered in a budget or the past year's transactions to fill in your average monthly spending.

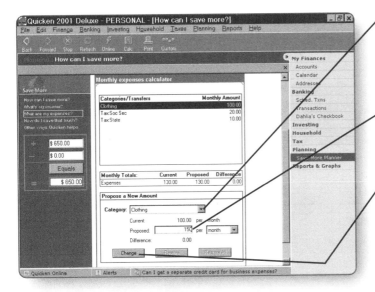

7. **Click** on a **category** for which you want to change the monthly amount. The category will be selected.

8. **Click** in the **Proposed text box** and **type** the **amount** you want to apply to the category.

9. **Click** on **Change**. The Monthly Amount field for the category will be updated.

You can also add categories to the Save More Planner.

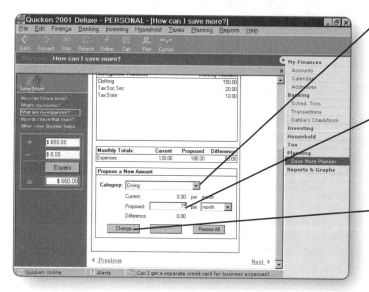

10. **Click** on the **Category down arrow** and **click** on the **category** that you want to add. The category will be selected.

11. **Click** in the **Proposed text box** and **type** the **amount** you will be spending on the category each month.

12. **Click** on **Change**. The category and monthly amount will be added to the list. You'll also notice that the Proposed amount will be changed.

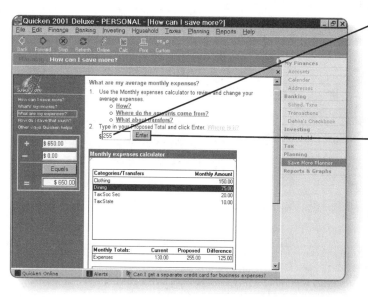

13. **Type** the **proposed amount** in the number 2 text box when you are finished adjusting the categories and amounts.

14. **Click** on **Enter**. The amount of your monthly expenses will appear in the calculator at the left of the screen.

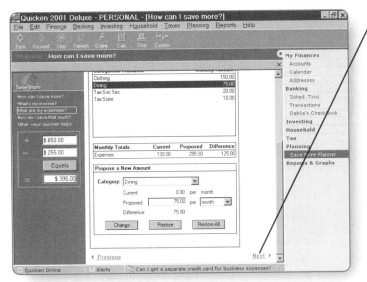

15. Click on **Next**. The How do I save that much? screen will appear.

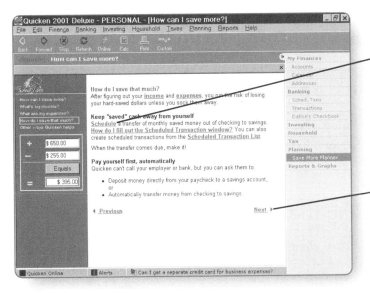

TIP

If you want to begin saving any residual money, you can have Quicken remind you to transfer the money to your savings account.

16. Click on **Next**. The Other ways Quicken can help you save screen will appear.

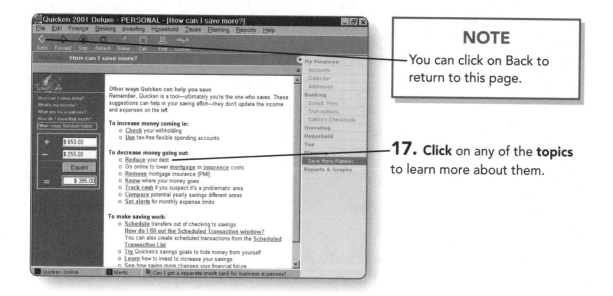

NOTE
You can click on Back to return to this page.

17. Click on any of the **topics** to learn more about them.

Establishing Savings Goals

Savings goals can help you set aside money for a particular purpose. Maybe you just need a few hundred dollars for a new scanner, a digital camera, or a color printer. Or, maybe you need a few thousand dollars to buy a second car. You have two different options to help you plan for a special purchase.

Using the Special Purchase Planner

If you are planning a special purchase in the future, such as a car, a wedding, or a new business, you may want to consider the Special Purchase Planner. This planner can help you if you think the purchase price might change before you have enough money saved. It is also useful if you will be borrowing money to finance part of the purchase.

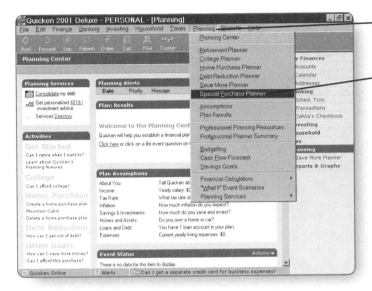

1. **Click** on **Planning**. The Planning menu will appear.

2. **Click** on **Special Purchase Planner**. The Special Purchase Planner will appear in the Planning window.

TIP

Another good way to save money is to reduce your debt. The Debt Reduction Planner has some good ideas and contains loads of information for reducing debt.

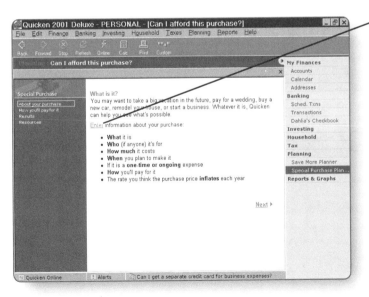

3. **Click** on the **Enter link**. The Add Special Expense dialog box will open.

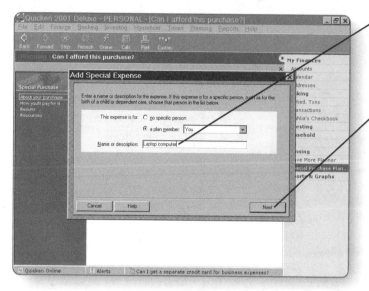

4. **Click** in the **Name or description text box** and **type** a **description** of the purchase that you want to make.

5. **Click** on **Next**. The next screen of the Add Special Expense dialog box will appear.

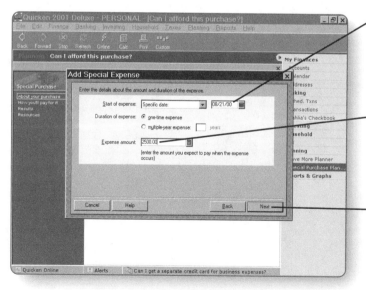

6. **Click** in the **Start of expense text box** and **type** the **date** on which you want to begin saving money for the purchase.

7. **Click** in the **Expense amount text box** and **type** the **amount** of the intended purchase.

8. **Click** on **Next**. The last screen of the Add Special Expense dialog box will appear.

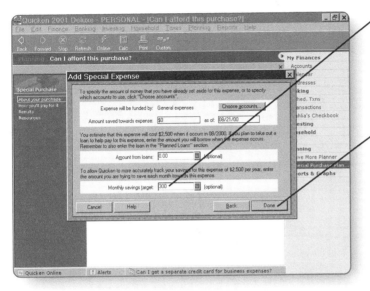

9. **Click** in the **Monthly savings target text box** and **type** the **amount** you want to set aside each month toward the purchase.

10. **Click** on **Done**. You will return to the Special Purchase Planner. You'll notice that the special expense has been added to the planner.

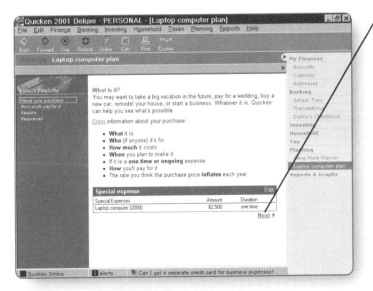

11. **Click** on **Next**. The How will you pay for it? screen of the planner will appear.

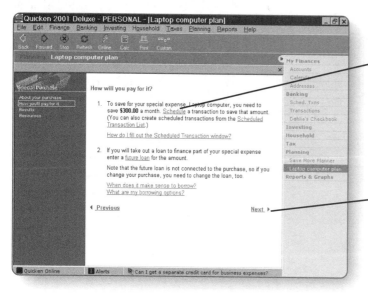

NOTE

You'll want to set up a scheduled transaction to transfer the amount into a savings account each month.

12. Click on **Next**. The Results screen of the planner will appear.

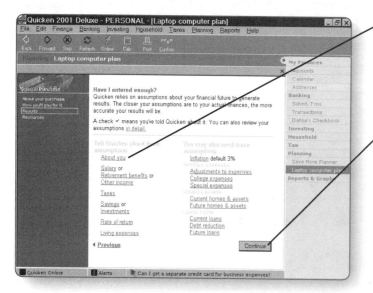

13. Click on a **link** to supply Quicken with more information so that the program can help guide you through the planning and savings process.

14. Click on **Continue**. The Resources for special purchases screen of the planner will appear.

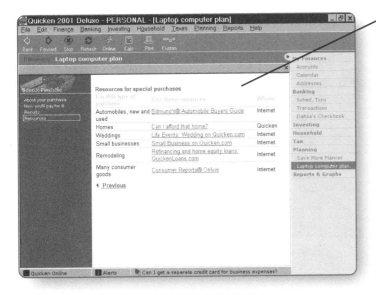

The resources page lists some places where you can find more information about saving for and making special purchases.

Working with Savings Goals

Another way to set money aside for a special purchase is to use savings goals. These goals help you decide how much you need to save and when you need to save it. You can then hide the savings amount away in your account register. When you've stashed away enough cash for the special purchase, it's time to go shopping!

Creating a Savings Goal Account

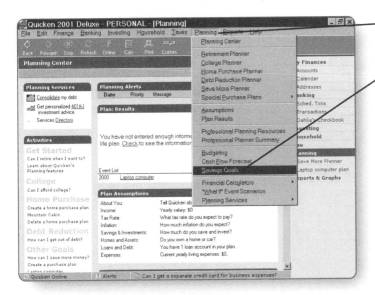

1. Click on **Planning**. The Planning menu will appear.

2. Click on **Savings Goals**. The Savings Goals will appear in the Planning window.

NOTE

You'll also find a link to the Savings Goals in the Other Activities area of the Planning Center.

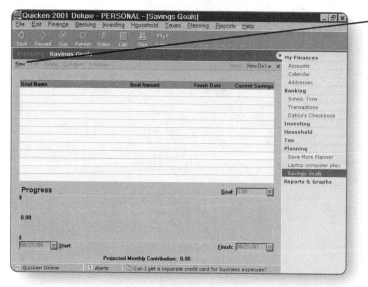

3. Click on **New**. The Create New Savings Goal dialog box will open.

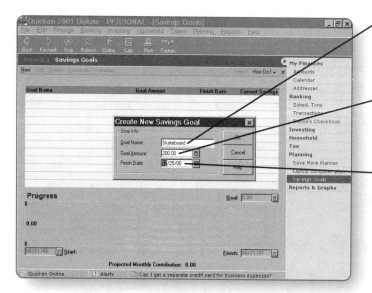

4. Click in the **Goal Name text box** and **type** a **name** to describe the goal.

5. Click in the **Goal Amount text box** and **type** the **amount** of money you want to save.

6. Click in the **Finish Date text box** and **type** the **date** on which you want to have accumulated the entire goal amount.

7. Click on **OK**. The new goal will appear in the Savings Goals list.

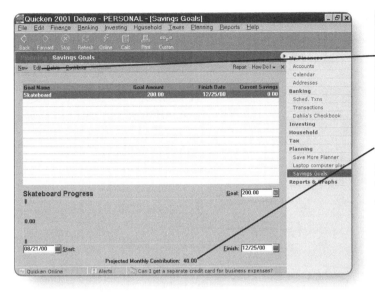

TIP

To make changes to the goal, select the goal and click on the Edit button.

At the bottom of the window, you'll find the amount of money that you'll need to contribute to the goal each month.

Contributing to Your Goal

Recording your contributions to your goal is also a simple process.

1. Click on the **goal** for which you want to set aside money. The goal will be selected.

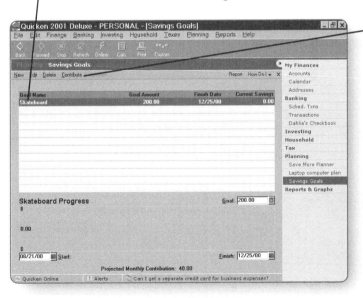

2. Click on **Contribute**. The Contribute To Goal dialog box will open.

3. Click on the **From Account down arrow** and **click** on the **account** from which you want to make the contribution to the goal. The account will appear in the list box.

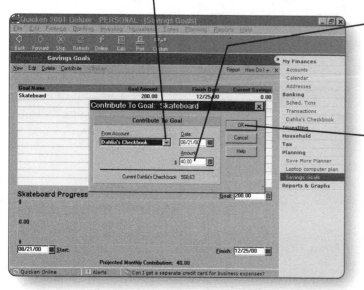

4. Click in the **Amount text box** and **type** the **amount** that you want to set aside for the goal, if it differs from the monthly average.

5. Click on **OK**. The contribution will be shown in the Savings Goals list and will also display in the register for the selected account.

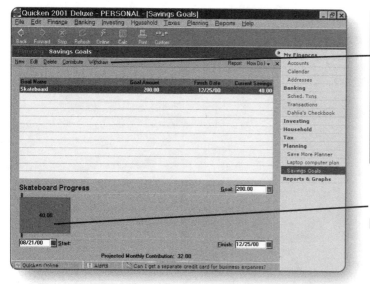

NOTE

When you have met the goal, you can withdraw the money from the savings goal account so that it is available to make the purchase.

Notice the progress bar at the bottom of the window.

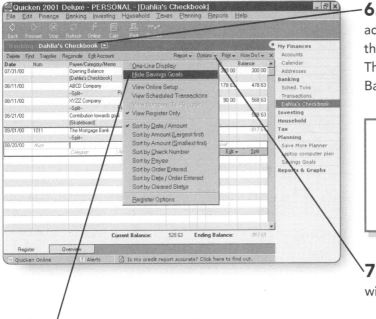

6. Display the **register** for the account from which you made the savings goal contribution. The register will appear in the Banking window.

NOTE

A transaction should appear in the register for the contribution, with the adjusted account balance.

7. Click on **Options**. A menu will appear.

8. Click on **Hide Savings Goals**. The transaction line for the contribution will be hidden.

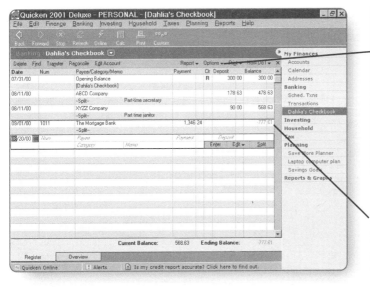

NOTE

To display the savings goal contributions in the register, click on Options and click on the Hide Savings Goals command from the menu that appears.

By hiding the contribution transactions, you show the actual balance of the account. The account no longer reflects any money set aside for the savings goals.

19

Investing in the Stock Market

One way to increase the value of your savings is to invest wisely. There are many ways to invest your money. You may want to put your money in a higher interest earning certificate of deposit. Or, you may choose to take a little more risk and invest in the stock market. Quicken can help you keep track of these investments so that you can keep your eye on your savings. In this chapter, you'll learn how to:

- Create accounts in which to track your investments
- Track the market prices of your investments
- View your portfolio's performance

Setting Up Investment Accounts

Quicken allows you to track many types of investments. But, before you can use Quicken's tracking features, you'll need to set up an account for each type of security in which you invest.

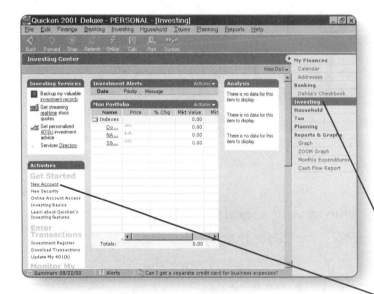

NOTE

As you work your way through the new account creation process, some of the screens displayed on your system may vary depending on options you selected.

1. **Click** on the **Investing QuickTab**. The Investing Center will appear.

2. **Click** on the **New Account link**. The Create New Account dialog box will open.

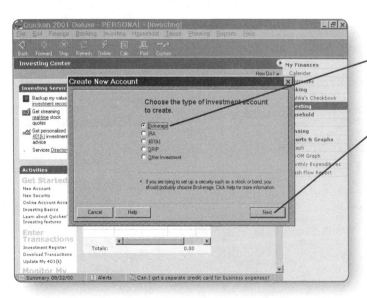

3. **Click** on the **Brokerage option button**. The option will be selected.

4. **Click** on **Next**. The About this account page will appear.

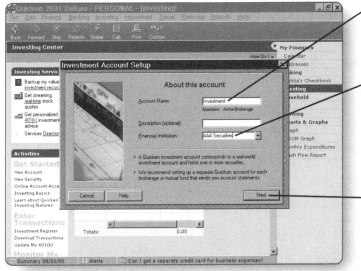

5. **Click** in the **Account Name text box** and **type** the **name** of the investment account.

6. **Click** in the **Financial Institution text box** and **type** the **name** of the investment firm where you trade your investment account.

7. **Click** on **Next**. The Does this investment account allow you to write checks or use a debit card against its balance? page will appear.

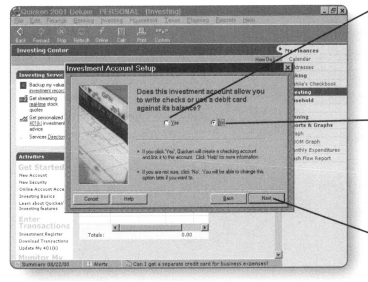

8a. **Click** on the **Yes option button** if you are able to write checks. The option will be selected.

OR

8b. **Click** on the **No option button** if you cannot withdraw cash from the investment account. The option will be selected.

9. **Click** on **Next**. The What kind of securities will this account contain? page will appear.

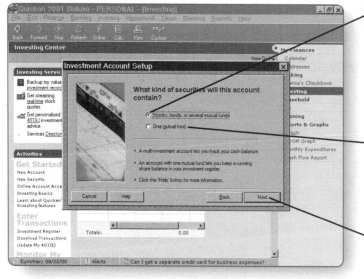

10a. **Click** on the **Stocks, bonds, or several mutual funds option button** if you have a diversified portfolio. The option will be selected.

OR

10b. **Click** on the **One mutual fund option button** if you have only invested in a single fund. The option will be selected.

11. **Click** on **Next**. The Enter the starting point information page will appear.

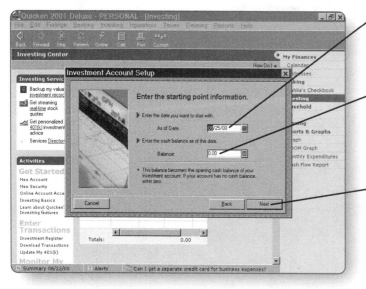

12. **Click** in the **As of Date text box** and **type** the **date** you opened the account.

13. **Click** in the **Balance text box** and **type** the **amount** of money you have placed in the account.

14. **Click** on **Next**. The Is this a tax-deferred or tax-exempt account? page will appear.

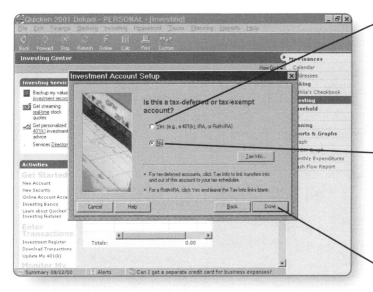

15a. Click on the **Yes option button** if the earnings from the account are tax-deferred or tax-exempt. The option will be selected.

OR

15b. Click on the **No option button** if the earnings from the account are subject to capital gains taxes. The option will be selected.

16. Click on **Done**. The What type of security would you like to create? page will appear.

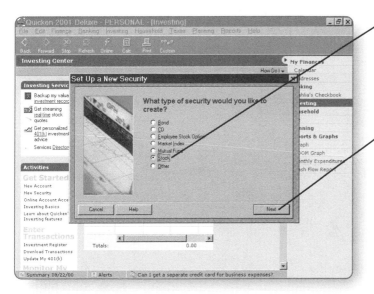

17. Click on the **option button** that corresponds to the type of investment that will be placed in the account. The option will be selected.

18. Click on **Next**. The What is the name of the new security? page will appear.

19. Click in the **Name text box** and **type** the **name** of the stock or mutual fund in which you have invested.

20. Click in the **Ticker Symbol text box** and **type** the **stock symbol** for the investment.

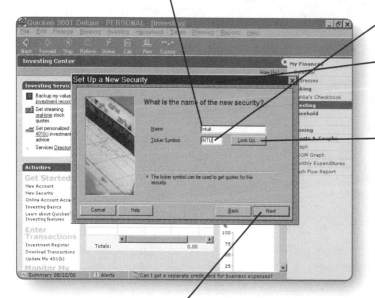

TIP

If you don't know the stock symbol, click on the Look Up button. You will be connected to the Internet and you can look for the symbol from the Quicken Web site.

21. Click on **Next**. The Asset classes and goals enhance Quicken's ability to analyze page will appear.

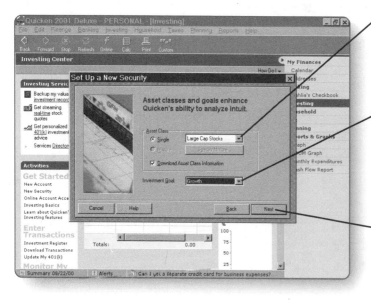

22. Click on the **Asset Class down arrow** and **select** the **class** of investment. The option will be selected.

23. Click on the **Investment Goal down arrow** and **select** the **reason** why you are investing in the stock market. The option will be selected.

24. Click on **Next**. The Quicken can track your cost basis one of two ways page will appear.

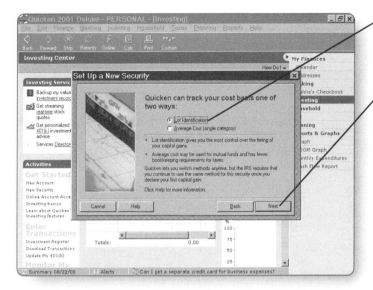

25. **Click** on the **Lot Identification option button**. The option will be selected.

26. **Click** on **Next**. The How do you want to track? page will appear.

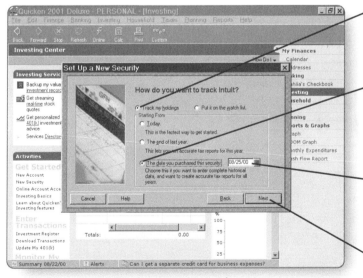

27. **Click** on the **Track my holdings option button**. The option will be selected.

28. **Click** on the **The date you purchased this security option button**. The option will be selected.

29. **Click** in the **date text box** and **type** the **date** on which you purchased the investment.

30. **Click** on **Next**. The Holdings page will appear.

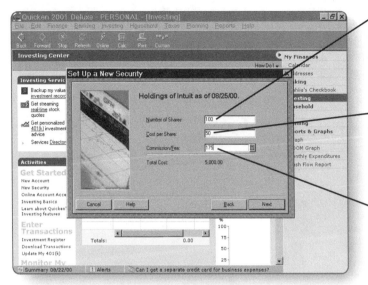

31. **Click** in the **Number of Shares text box** and **type** the **number** of shares of stock you purchased.

32. **Click** in the **Cost per Share text box** and **type** the **price** you paid for each share of stock.

33. **Click** in the **Commission/Fee text box** and **type** the **amount** of commission that you were charged by the investment firm for executing the transaction.

34. **Click** on **Next**. The You are about to create the new security page will appear.

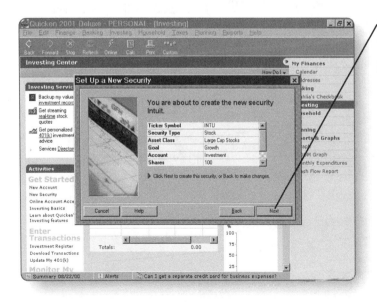

35. **Click** on **Next**. The The security has been set up page will appear.

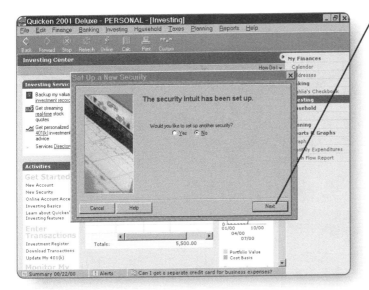

36. **Click** on **Next** if you do not want to add any other stock investments to the account. The Get a headstart by downloading asset classes and historical prices page will appear.

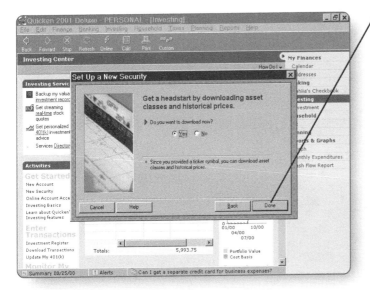

37. **Click** on **Done**. The Quicken Download Status dialog box will open.

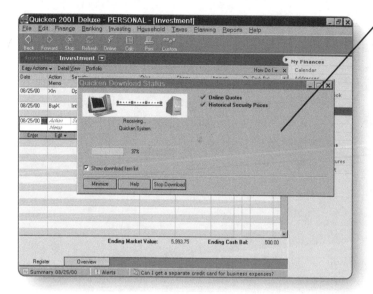

38. **Wait** while **Quicken downloads** the historical prices. The Quicken Download Summary dialog box will open.

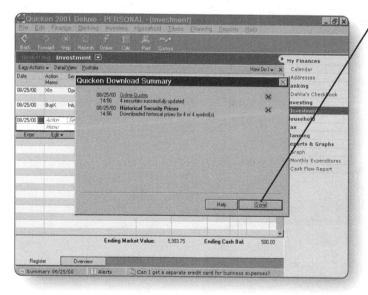

39. **Click** on **Done**. The Investment Register will appear.

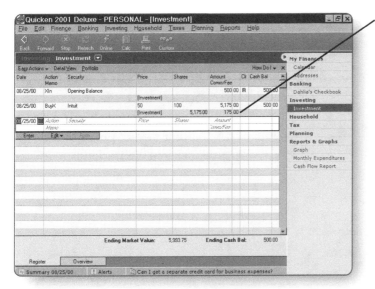

The Investment register works much like the other registers that you've seen. When you buy or sell an investment, record the information in the register.

Tracking Market Prices

When you want to see how well your investments are performing, you can ask Quicken to look up the information for you.

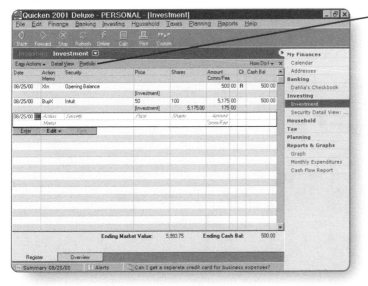

1. **Click** on the **Portfolio button**. The Portfolio View will appear.

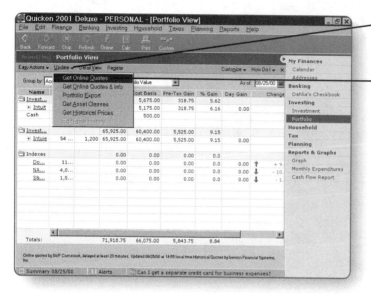

2. Click on **Update**. A menu will appear.

3. Click on **Get Online Quotes**. Quicken will connect to the Internet and download the current market prices of the stock you are tracking.

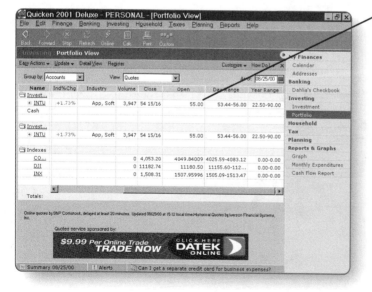

The Portfolio View tells you the opening and closing price of the stock, the price range for the day, and the high and low prices for the current year.

Viewing Your Portfolio

When you want a graphical representation of how well your portfolio is performing, take a look at the Investment Performance Graph.

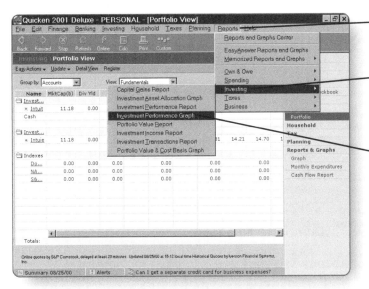

1. Click on **Reports**. The Reports menu will appear.

2. Move the **mouse pointer** to Investing. A second menu will appear.

3. Click on **Investment Performance Graph**. The Investment Performance Graph will appear.

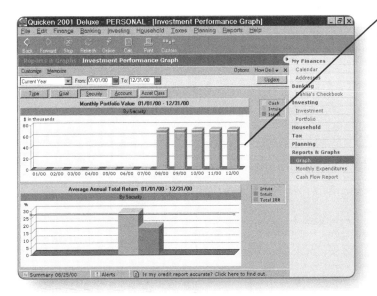

The graph shows the value of the portfolio by month and the percent return you have earned on the investments.

Part V Review Questions

1. What is the best way to keep track of where you spend your earnings? *See "Building a Budget" in Chapter 17*

2. How can Quicken make it easy for you to stay within your budget? *See "Setting Budget Alerts" in Chapter 17*

3. What reports can you generate so that you can see how well you are meeting your budget goals? *See "Staying on Budget" in Chapter 17*

4. Which Quicken feature shows you where you can save additional money? *See "Learning to Save" in Chapter 18*

5. How can you decide if you might be able to set aside money for a special purchase? *See "Establishing Savings Goals" in Chapter 18*

6. How do you set up an account so that you can save money for a special purchase? *See "Using the Special Purchase Planner" in Chapter 18*

7. How do you set aside money for a special purchase? *See "Working with Savings Goals" in Chapter 18*

8. What are the different types of investment accounts that can be tracked in Quicken? *See "Setting Up Investment Accounts" in Chapter 19*

9. How can Quicken help you automatically track the value of your portfolio? *See "Tracking Market Prices" in Chapter 19*

10. What is the easiest way to see how well your portfolio is performing? *See "Viewing Your Portfolio" in Chapter 19*

PART VI

Planning for Major Expenses

20

Saving for College

You're never too young or too old to think about going to
college, junior college, business college, or vocational school.
To pursue your interests or gain skills to help advance your
career, you'll want to plan for college tuition, books, housing,
and other expenses. Quicken contains two tools that can help
you make those important college financial planning decisions.
The College Calculator is a simple tool if you're looking for
some quick numbers to use for planning purposes. The College
Planner provides advice and information on how much college
is going to cost and how to pay for it. In this chapter, you'll
learn how to:

- Use the College Calculator to determine how much you'll
  need to set aside to pay for a college education

- Work with the College Planner to build a long-term plan to
  finance a college education

Determining College Costs

The College Calculator is a great way to work out a number of scenarios to determine college costs and annual contributions to a college savings account.

Computing a Lump Sum Contribution

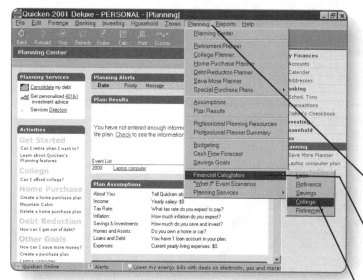

If you know what a college education will cost, you can use the College Calculator to determine how much you will need to invest in a college savings account in one lump sum in order to be able to pay those college costs as they occur.

1. Click on **Planning**. The Planning menu will appear.

2. Move the **mouse pointer** to Financial Calculators. A submenu will appear.

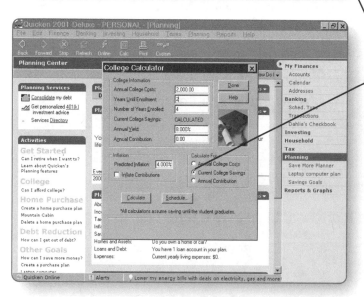

3. Click on **College**. The College Calculator will appear.

4. Click on the **Current College Savings option button**. The option will be selected.

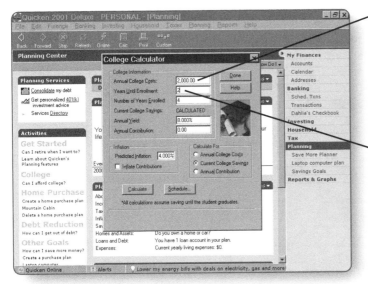

5. Click in the **Annual College Costs text box** and **type** the **amount** you estimate will be needed to cover college costs for a year. The amount will appear in the text box.

6. Click in the **Years Until Enrollment text box** and **type** the **number** of years it will be before the college education will start.

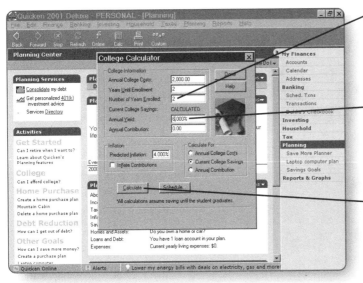

7. Click in the **Number of Years Enrolled text box** and **type** the **number** of years that the college education will last.

8. Click in the **Annual Yield text box** and **type** the **interest rate** you expect to earn on the college savings account.

9. Click on the **Calculate button**. The starting college savings amount will be calculated.

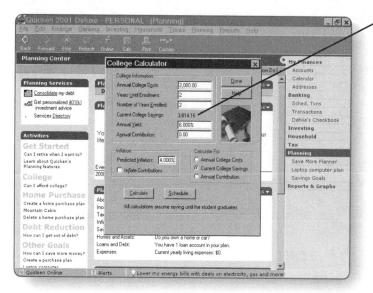

You'll find the amount you'll need to invest as a lump sum in order to be able to pay the estimated college costs in the Current College Savings field.

Computing an Annual Savings Amount

If you know how much the college education will cost, you can calculate how much you'll need to save each year to be able to pay those costs.

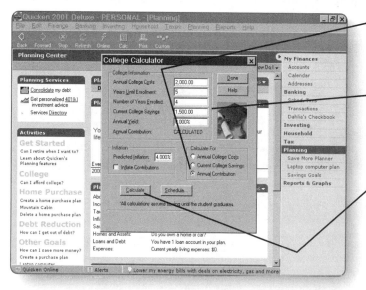

1. Click on the **Annual Contribution option button**. The option will be selected.

2. Click in each **text box**, in turn, in the College Information section and **type** the **required information**.

3. Click on the **Calculate button**. The annual savings amount will be calculated.

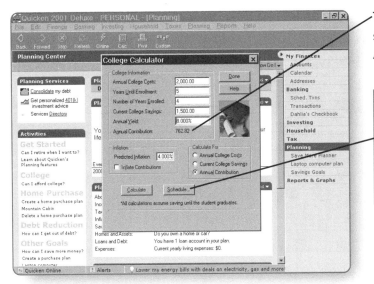

The amount that you'll need to save each year will appear in the Annual Contribution field.

TIP

You can print a schedule of the deposits you'll need to make. Just click on the Schedule button.

Determining College Spending Limits

If you have some money set aside and are able to set aside an additional amount every year for a college education, you can determine how much you will have when it comes time for you or your kids to go off to college.

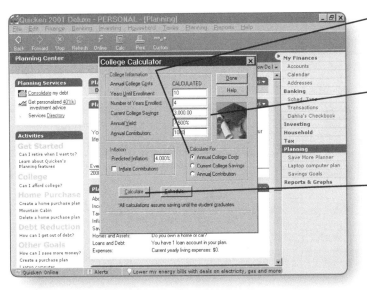

1. **Click** on the **Annual College Costs option button**. The option will be selected.

2. **Click** in each **text box**, in turn, in the College Information section and **type** the **required information** in the text boxes.

3. **Click** on the **Calculate button**. The annual college spending limit will be calculated.

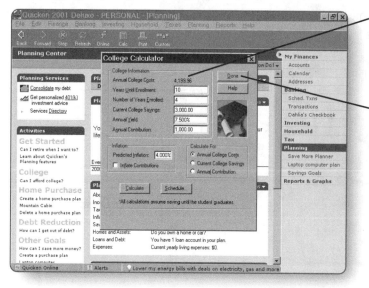

You'll find the amount that you can spend each year for college costs in the Annual College Costs field.

4. Click on **Done** when you are finished with the College Calculator. The calculator will close.

Using the College Planner

If you want to work out a long-term, flexible plan for funding a college education, but you don't want to pay a professional planner for assistance, use the services of the College Planner.

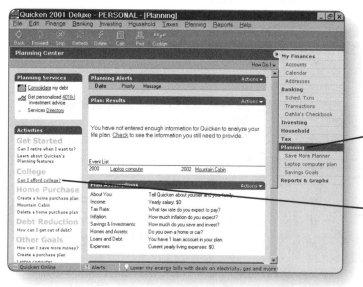

The planner contains an abundance of guidance and ideas. The College Planner is a powerful tool, and the instructions that follow are just an introduction to get you started.

1. Click on the **Planning QuickTab**. The Planning Center will appear.

2. Click on the **Can I afford college? link**. The Welcome page of the College Planner will appear in the Planning window.

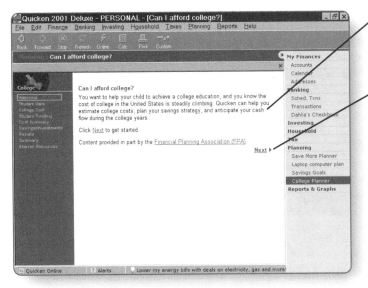

3. **Read** each **page** of the planner carefully before you proceed to the next page.

4. **Click** on the **Next link**. The Student Data page of the College Planner will appear.

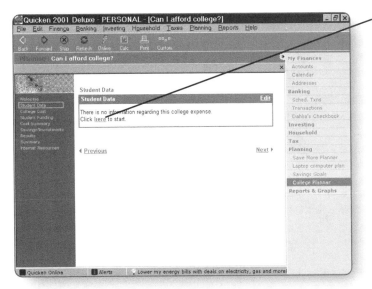

5. **Click** on the **Click here to start link**. A dialog box will open.

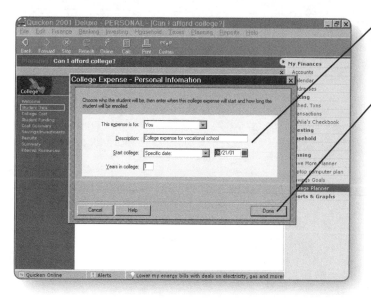

6. **Enter** the **appropriate information** in each of the text fields.

7. **Click** on **Done**. You will return to the College Planner.

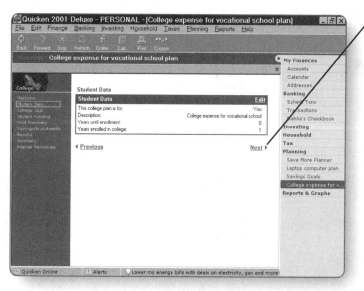

8. **Continue** through the **College Planner**. Remember to read the directions, type the appropriate information, and click on the Next link to continue. You will come to the Results page.

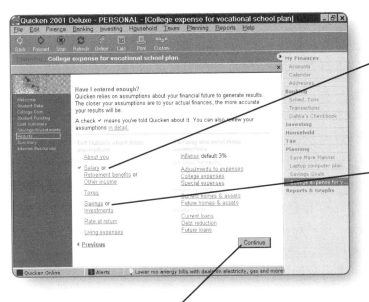

NOTE

For those assumptions that you've completed, a check mark will appear next to the link.

9. **Click** on a **link** in the Tell Quicken about these assumptions area. The more information Quicken has, the better it can help you. A dialog box will open.

10. **Click** on the **Continue button**. The Summary page will appear.

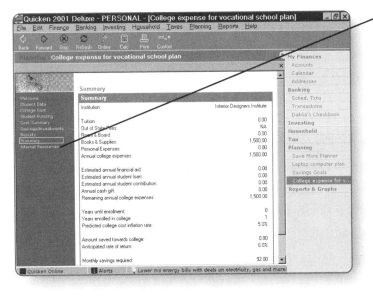

11. **Click** on **Internet Resources**. The Internet Resources page will appear.

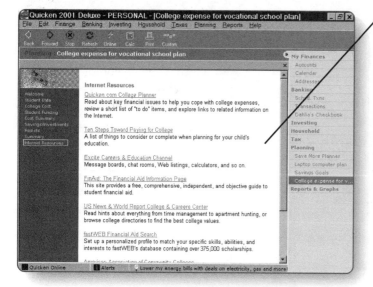

This page contains a number of resources for the college-bound.

21

Buying a Car

Dreaming about a new car can be fun, but if you base you car-buying decision on a dream, you may not be happy with the reality. If you think you've found the perfect car, do a little research and see if the car measures up to your expectations (and your pocketbook). Quicken has teamed up with Edmunds to provide car pricing, reviews, and other information to help you make your decision. Edmunds has been publishing vehicle prices and reviews since 1966. To purchase the car, you'll need to pay cash or obtain a loan. It also is a good idea to track your automobile expenses. In this chapter, you'll learn how to:

- Find a one-stop information bank for car shoppers
- Make a car-financing decision
- Track car expenses

Making Car Purchase Decisions

How do you really know if you're getting the best car value for your money? Edmunds' Web site is a helpful guide (http://www.edmunds.com); it's easy to navigate and contains a wealth of information.

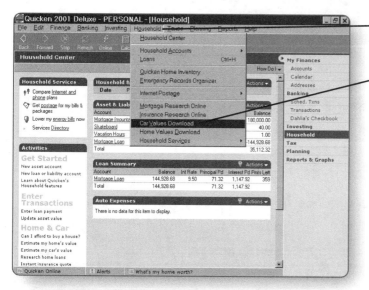

1. **Click** on **Household**. The Household menu will appear.

2. **Click** on **Car Values Download**. The Estimate the value of your car page will appear in the Household window.

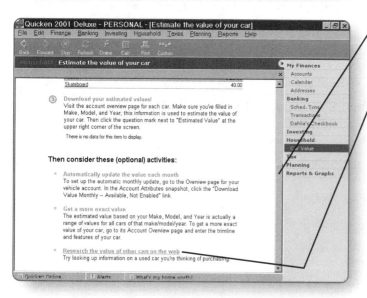

3. **Scroll** to the **bottom** of the page. You'll see a list of optional activities.

4. **Click** on the **Research the value of other cars on the web link**. You'll be taken to Edmunds' Automotive Information Source for Quicken page.

Edmunds is a good place to start car shopping because you can sit in one place and find loads of new and used automobile information.

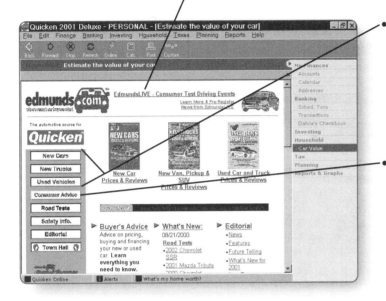

- **New Cars, New Trucks, and Used Vehicles.** These links provide specifications and prices, reviews, insurance estimates, warranty information, and directions to a car dealer near you.

- **Consumer Advice**. Before you start car shopping, check out the Consumer Advice link. You'll find help and advice on shopping for a car, leasing a vehicle, and dealing with used car salesmen. A search feature allows you to find the history of a particular car and much more.

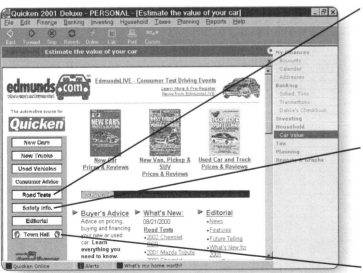

- **Road Tests**. If you really want to know about a car's performance, check out the Road Tests link. You can read a number of reviews and comparison tests and find Edmunds' favorite picks.

- **Safety Info**. Hang out with the crash test dummies at the Safety Info link. You'll find crash test data, manufacturer recalls, and other car safety information.

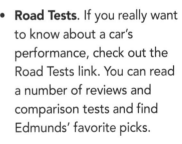

- **Town Hall**. If you're curious about what others have to say about cars, sign up at the Town Hall and chat with other car owners about their cars and related issues.

Calculating Car Loan Payments

If you can't pay cash for a car, you need to consider financing options. Determine what the monthly payments would be and how they relate to your budget. Don't forget to consider other car expenses, such as gasoline, parking fees, car insurance, and maintenance.

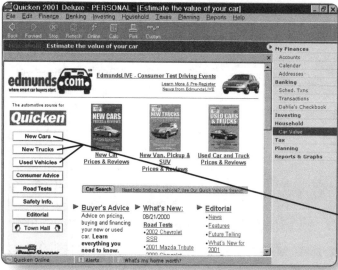

Visiting CarFinance.com

An Auto Loan Calculator appears at the bottom of each of the car information pages at the Edmunds Web site. Another loan calculator is hidden away in Edmunds' pages. Here's where you'll find Edmunds' calculators.

1. Click on the **link** for New Cars, New Trucks, or Used Vehicles. A list of car manufacturers will appear.

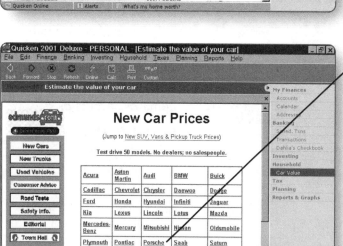

2. Click on the **manufacturer** of the car that you are interested in buying. A list of car models will appear.

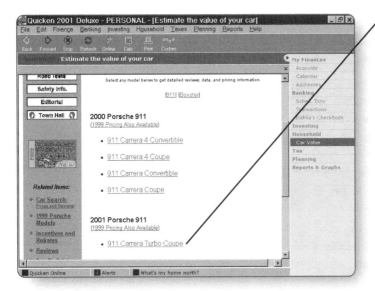

3. **Click** on a **model**. The information page for the automobile will appear.

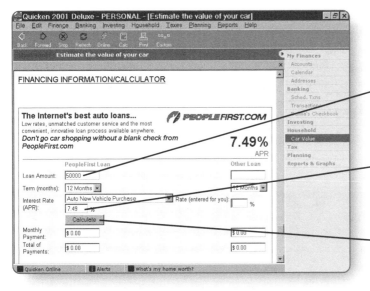

4. **Scroll** to the **bottom of the page**. The Auto Loan Calculator will appear.

5. **Click** in the **Loan Amount text box** and **type** the **amount** you want to finance.

6. **Click** in the **Interest Rate (APR) text box** for your rate and **type** an **interest rate**.

7. **Click** on the **Calculate button**. The Auto Loan Calculator will compute the loan payment.

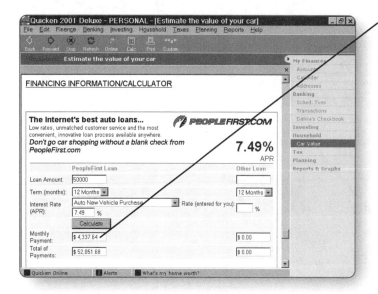

The Auto Loan Calculator calculates loan payments based on loans of 12 to 72 months' duration.

> ### NOTE
> You can use the rest of the calculator to see special financing terms available from PeopleFirst.com and also apply for a car loan.

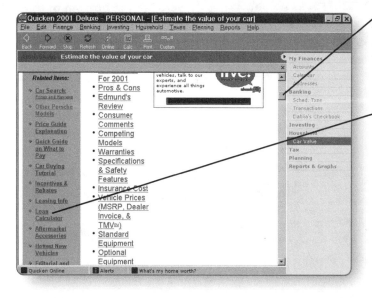

8. Scroll toward the **top** of the page. You'll see the navigation bar along the left side of the page.

9. Click on the **Loan Calculator link**. The Loan Calculator page will appear.

10. Click in the **Price of Car text box** and **type** the **price** you expect to pay for the vehicle. Do not use commas.

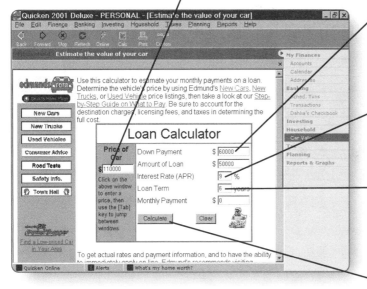

11. Click in the **Down Payment text box** and **type** the **amount** you'll be paying out of pocket for the vehicle.

12. Click in the **Interest Rate (APR) text box** and **type** the **interest rate** you expect to pay.

13. Click in the **Loan Term text box** and **type** the **number** of years for which you want to finance the vehicle.

14. Click on the **Calculate button**. The monthly payment will be calculated.

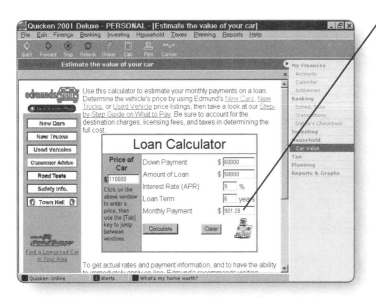

The car payment will appear in the Monthly Payment text box.

NOTE

If the monthly payment is too high, you may need to check for a better interest rate or loan term.

Using the Quicken Loan Calculator

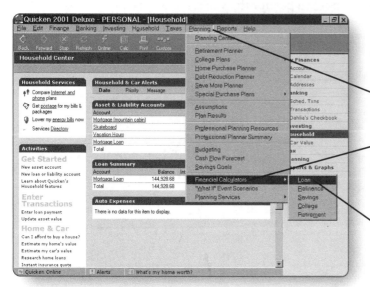

Quicken can also help you calculate loan payments. Just follow a few simple steps.

1. Click on **Planning**. The Planning menu will appear.

2. Move the **mouse pointer** to Financial Calculators. A submenu will appear.

3. Click on **Loan**. The Loan Calculator will appear.

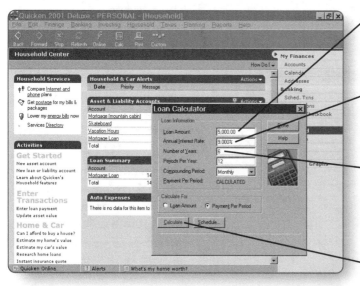

4. Click in the **Loan Amount text box** and **type** the **amount** that you want to finance.

5. Click in the **Annual Interest Rate text box** and **type** the **interest rate** you expect to pay.

6. Click in the **Number of Years text box** and **type** the **number of years** that you will be paying on the loan.

7. Click on the **Calculate button**. The monthly loan payment will be calculated.

You'll find the monthly payment amount in the Payment Per Period field.

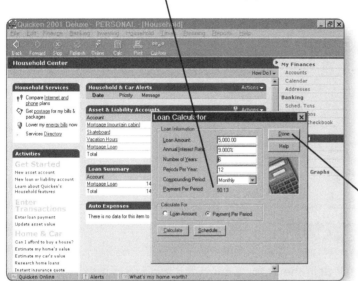

NOTE

You can try out other scenarios by changing the information in the text boxes and clicking on the Calculate button.

8. Click on **Done** when you are finished with the calculator. The calculator will close.

Tracking Car Expenses

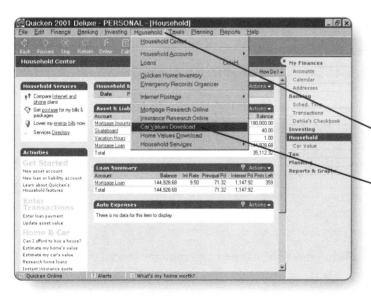

Quicken makes it easy to keep track of your car as an asset account and your automobile loan as a liability account. Let the wizard show you the steps.

1. Click on **Household**. The Household menu will appear.

2. Click on **Car Values Download**. The Find out how much your car is worth! page will appear in the Household window.

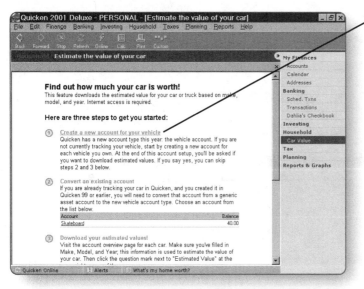

3. **Click** on the **Create a new account for your vehicle link**. The Asset Account Setup wizard will start and the About this car/vehicle page will be displayed.

4. **Click** in the **Enter a name for this account text box** and **type** a **name** for the car account.

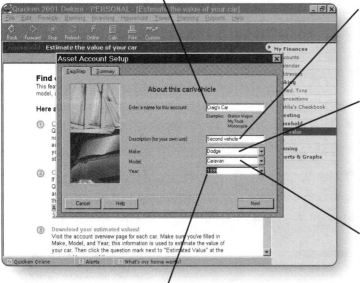

5. **Click** in the **Description (for your own use) text box** and **type** a **description** of the car or its use.

6. **Click** in the **Make text box** and **type** the **manufacturer** of the car. The wizard will attempt to help you fill in this field. Keep typing until you see the correct name.

7. **Click** in the **Model text box** and **type** the **car model**.

8. **Click** in the **Year text box** and **type** the **model year** of the car.

9. **Click** on **Next**. The Enter the starting point information page will appear.

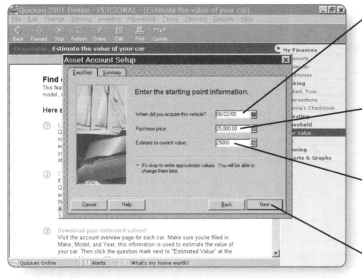

10. Click in the **When did you acquire this vehicle? text box** and **type** the **date** on which you purchased the car.

11. Click in the **Purchase price text box** and **type** the **total amount** you paid for the car.

12. Click in the **Estimate its current value text box** and **type** the **resale value** of the car.

13. Click on **Next**. The Is there a loan on this vehicle? page will appear.

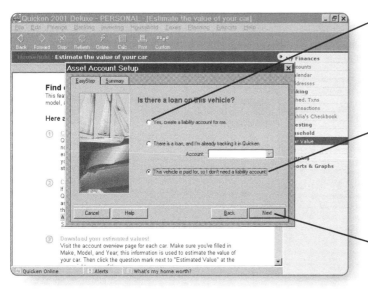

14a. If you financed the car, **click** on the **option button** for Yes, create a liability account for me. The option will be selected.

OR

14b. If the car is paid off, **click** on the **option button** for This vehicle is paid for, so I don't need a liability account. The option will be selected.

15. Click on **Next**. The Summary page will appear.

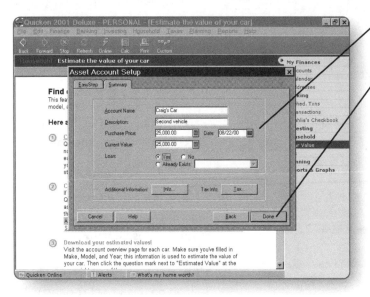

16. Verify that the **information** is correct.

17. Click on **Done**. If you financed the car, the Edit Loan wizard will start.

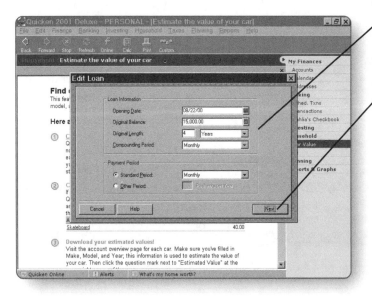

18. Type the **information** about the loan in the appropriate text boxes.

19. Click on **Next**. The next page of the Edit Loan wizard will appear.

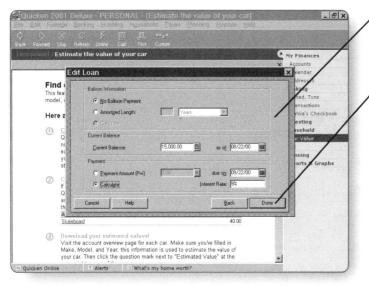

20. Type the **information** about the loan in the appropriate text boxes.

21. Click on **Done**. The Edit Loan Payment dialog box will open.

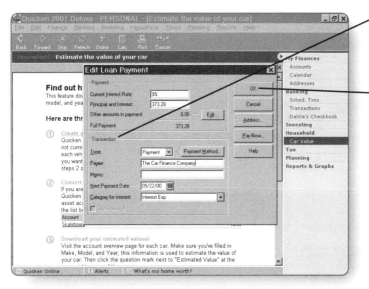

22. Type the **information** about the loan payment in the Transaction section.

23. Click on **OK**. A confirmation dialog box will open.

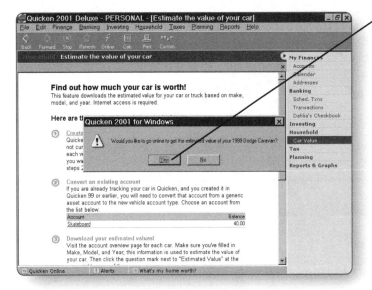

24. Click on **Yes**. The current market value for your automobile will be updated in your Quicken records.

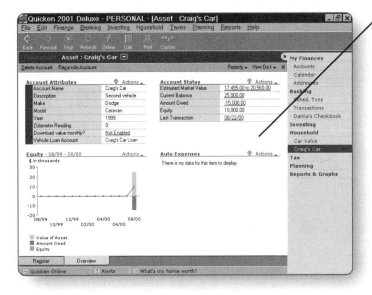

You now have everything you need to keep track of your car's value and your automobile loan.

22

Owning a Home

Buying a home is a major decision for most people. There are so many decisions to make just about the house itself: the location, the number of bedrooms, the size of the yard—and that's only the beginning. Unfortunately, the major factor in deciding what kind of house to buy is usually the price. Before you go house hunting, check out Quicken's home purchase tools: a calculator to help you determine monthly mortgage payments, a planner to guide you through the home buying process, and even a Web site. In this chapter, you'll learn how to:

- Calculate how much you can afford to borrow
- Find the services provided by the Home Purchase Planner
- Find mortgage information and lenders on the Web

Calculating Your Mortgage Budget

If you're looking for an easy way to do a few mortgage calculations, start with the Loan Calculator. The Loan Calculator can estimate a monthly mortgage payment based on the loan and interest rate you will be paying. It can also determine the maximum mortgage loan you can afford based on what you want to pay as a monthly payment.

TIP

When estimating the mortgage payment, don't forget to add the cost of homeowner's insurance and property taxes. You may also want to add something extra to help cover maintenance costs such as replacing the roof, painting the house, or converting to solar power.

Estimating Monthly Mortgage Payments

If you've found a house you really like, but aren't sure if you'll be able to afford the monthly payments, try a few calculations with the Loan Calculator. Tell the Loan Calculator how much you plan to borrow and the interest rate you expect to pay. The Loan Calculator will then tell you what you can expect to pay for a monthly mortgage payment.

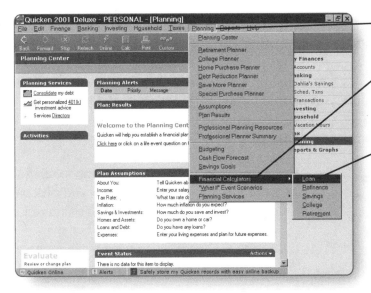

1. Click on **Planning**. The Planning menu will appear.

2. Move the **mouse pointer** to Financial Calculators. A submenu will appear.

3. Click on **Loan**. The Loan Calculator will appear.

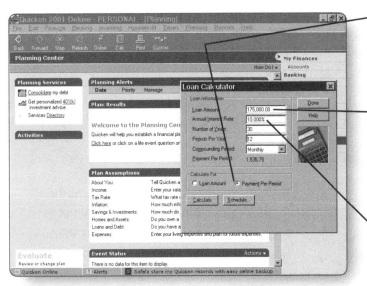

4. Click on the **Payment Per Period option button**, if it is not already selected. The option will be selected.

5. Click in the **Loan Amount text box** and **type** the **amount** of the mortgage loan. This is the purchase price of the home less your down payment.

6. Click in the **Annual Interest Rate text box** and **type** the **interest rate** you expect to pay on the mortgage loan.

NOTE

If you'll be working with an adjustable rate loan, enter the beginning interest rate.

7. Click in the **Number of Years text box** and **type** the **number** of years you will be paying on the loan.

8. Click in the **Periods Per Year text box** and **type** the **number** of payments you'll make each year.

9. Click on the **Compounding Period down arrow** and **click** on the **frequency** at which interest will be compounded on the loan. The frequency will appear in the list box.

10. Click on **Calculate**. The monthly payment will be calculated.

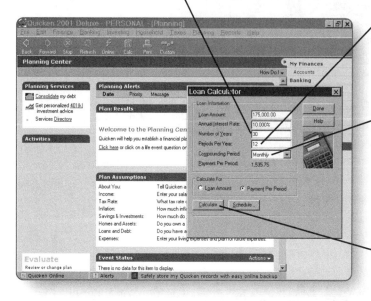

The amount of the loan payment will appear in the Payment Per Period field.

11. Click on the **Schedule button**. The Approximate Future Payment Schedule will appear.

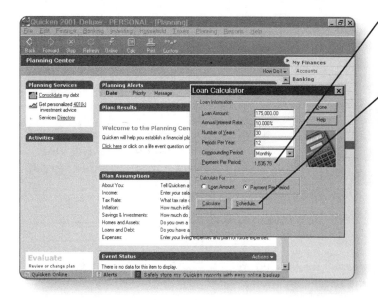

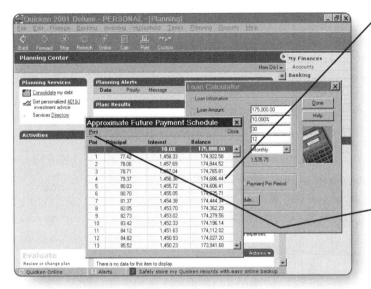

The Approximate Future Payment Schedule shows the principal and interest payments during the life of the loan. You'll notice that after each payment, the balance of the loan is reduced.

TIP

If you want a paper copy of the payment schedule, click on Print.

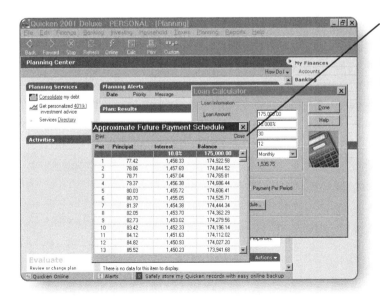

12. Click on the **Close button**. The Approximate Future Payment Schedule will close and you'll return to the Loan Calculator.

Estimating the Loan Amount

If you know how much you can afford to pay each month in mortgage payments, the Loan Calculator can determine the amount you can afford to borrow to purchase a home. The down payment that you will need to buy a house is the difference between the mortgage loan amount and the purchase price of the house.

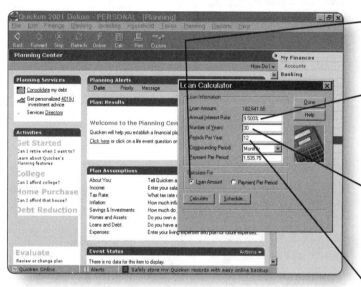

1. **Click** on the **Loan Amount option button**. The option will be selected.

2. **Click** in the **Annual Interest Rate text box** and **type** the **interest rate** you expect to pay on the mortgage loan.

3. **Click** in the **Number of Years text box** and **type** the **number** of years you will be paying on the loan.

4. **Click** in the **Periods Per Year text box** and **type** the **number** of payments you will be making each year.

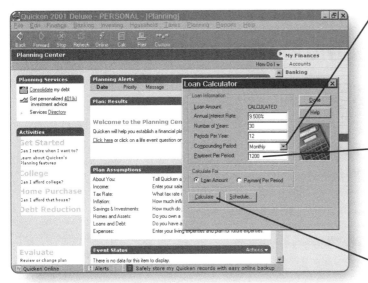

5. Click on the **Compounding Period down arrow** and **click** on the **frequency** at which interest will be compounded on the loan. The frequency will appear in the list box.

6. Click in the **Payment Per Period text box** and **type** the **amount** you can afford to pay each month for a mortgage payment.

7. Click on **Calculate**. The loan amount will be calculated.

The amount of the loan that you can afford will appear in the Loan Amount field.

8. Click on **Done** when you are finished using the calculator. The calculator will close.

Consulting the Home Purchase Planner

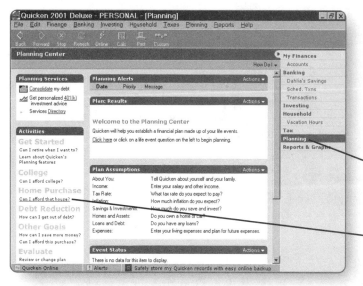

If you feel you need a guided approach to making a home purchase decision, the Home Purchase Planner is worth a look. You'll feel like you're working with a seasoned pro as you click your way through the planner.

1. Click on the **Planning QuickTab**. The Planning Center window will appear.

2. Click on the **Can I afford that house? link**. The Home Purchase Planner will appear in the Planning window.

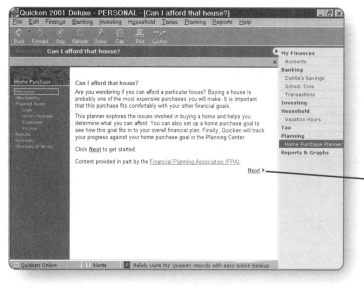

The Home Purchase Planner works like the other planners that you've seen used in this book. Take your time when working through the planner. There's a lot of information for you to read and many questions to answer.

3. Click on the **Next link**. The next page of the planner will appear.

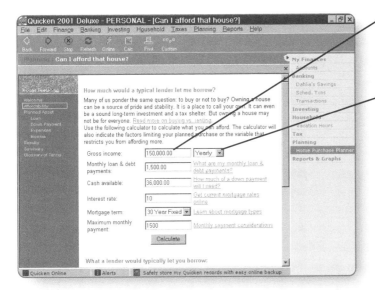

4. **Click** in the **text boxes** and **type** the **information** needed by the planner.

5. **Click** on the **list box down arrows**. Drop-down lists will appear.

6. **Click** to make a **selection** from the drop-down lists. The selections will be highlighted.

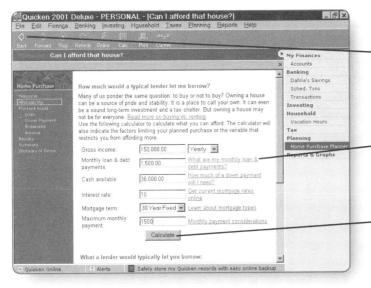

NOTE

Click on Back to return to the page you were viewing.

7. **Click** on a **link**. A page will appear that contains more information.

8. **Click** on the **Calculate button**. The information that you entered will be submitted to the planner.

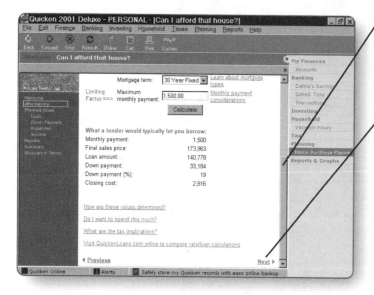

9. Scroll to the **bottom** of the page. You'll see the results of the information that you entered into the planner.

10. Click on the **Next link**. The Planned Asset page will appear.

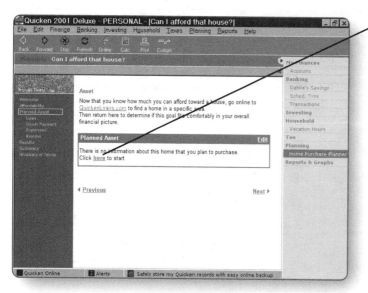

11. Click on the **Click here to start link**. The Add Planned Asset wizard will start.

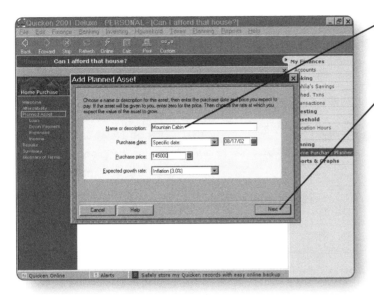

12. Click in the **text boxes** and **type** the requested **information**.

13. Click on **Next**. The next page of the wizard will appear.

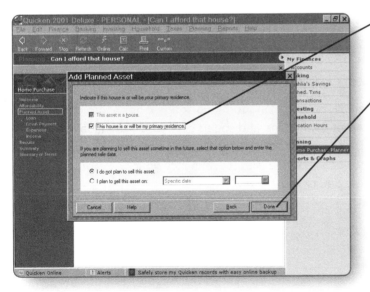

14. Answer each **question**. The options you choose will be selected.

15. Click on **Done**. You will return to the planner.

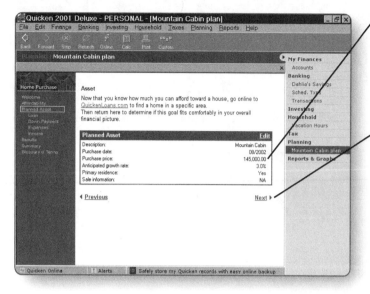

You'll see the information about the house you intend to buy in the Planned Asset section. If you want to change this information, click on the Edit link.

16. **Click** on **Next** and continue working with the planner. When you get to the Summary page, you'll see how well you'll be able to afford your planned dream home.

Researching Mortgage Rates on the Web

Well, it's time to do a little shopping from the comfort of your chair. If you're looking for a mortgage lender, turn on your Internet connection and speed over to QuickenLoans.com. This site is not just for first-time home buyers. It is also a good place to visit if you want to refinance your home or take out a home equity loan.

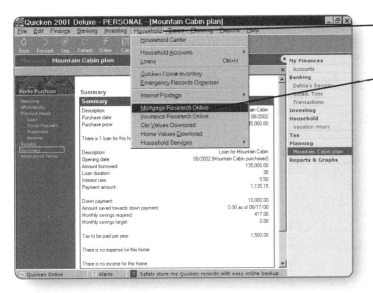

1. Click on **Household**. The Household menu will appear.

2. Click on **Mortgage Research Online**. The QuickenLoans.com page will appear in the Household Center window.

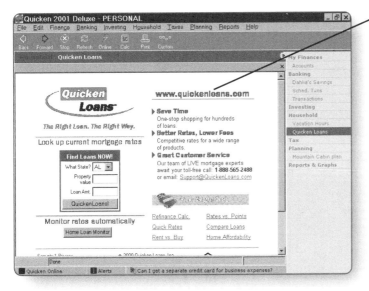

3. Click on the **links** to visit the different areas at QuickenLoans.com. You'll find an abundance of tools at this site: interest rate charts, loan comparisons, credit assessments, online applications, listings of homes for sale, and more. Have fun exploring and learning!

23

Planning for Retirement

If you want to enjoy a comfortable retirement with enough income to meet your needs, you need to begin planning early. The sooner you begin your retirement plan and start saving, the more money you'll have when you retire. Your retirement income level will depend on the soundness of your investment plan, how much money you invest, and how well you stick to the plan. Of course, you will need to adjust the plan along the way. Quicken contains two useful retirement planning tools. The Retirement Calculator can help you make some quick calculations, and the Retirement Planner can help you build a sound, long-term retirement plan. If you need professional financial help, Quicken can help you find a Certified Financial Planner. In this chapter, you'll learn how to:

- Perform calculations to determine how much you'll need to save to achieve your desired retirement income

- Enlist the professional help of the Retirement Planner to put together a comprehensive retirement plan

- Find a professional financial planner in your area to help you achieve your financial goals

Using the Retirement Calculator

You've seen a few financial calculators in the last few chapters of this book. The Retirement Calculator works much the same way as these other financial calculators. You tell the calculator what to compute, you type in a few numbers, and the calculator does its job. When you want to create a few quick retirement scenarios, the Retirement Calculator is the tool to choose.

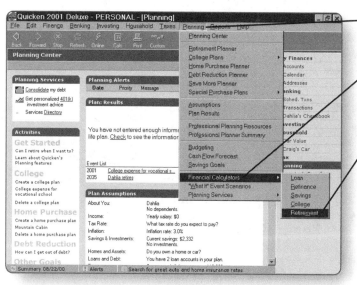

1. Click on **Planning**. The Planning menu will appear.

2. Move the **mouse pointer** to Financial Calculators. A submenu will appear.

3. Click on **Retirement**. The Retirement Calculator will appear.

4. Click on an **option button** to select one of the retirement calculations. The option will be selected. You can perform three different calculations.

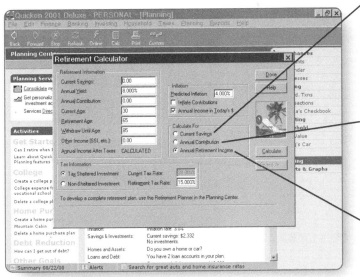

- **Current Savings**. If you want to know how much money you need to have currently in savings in order to attain your retirement income goals, click on this option button.

- **Annual Contribution**. To determine how much you need to save each year in order to reach your retirement goal, click on this option button.

- **Annual Retirement Income**. If you want to know how much retirement income your current savings will provide, click on this option button.

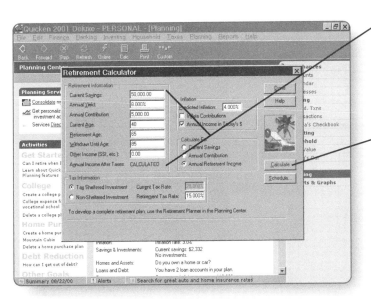

5. Click in each of the **text boxes** in the Retirement Information section and **type** the **information** needed by the calculator

6. Click on the **Calculate button**. The calculator will perform the math for you.

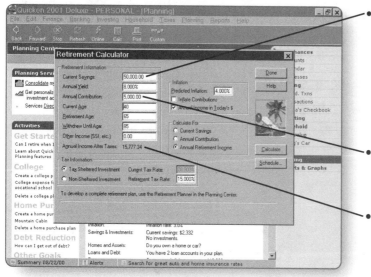

- If you selected the Current Savings option button, you'll see the amount you need to have currently in savings in the Current Savings field of the Retirement Information section.

- The Annual Contribution calculation is found in the Annual Contribution field.

- The Annual Retirement Income calculation is found in the Annual Income After Taxes field.

7. Click on **Done** when you are finished with the calculator.

Creating a Retirement Plan

You've already seen some of the planners that are found in Quicken. The Retirement Planner works the same way as other planners, but may take more time. If you've been keeping your records in Quicken, you'll see much of the information filled out for you. You can always add and edit information as needed.

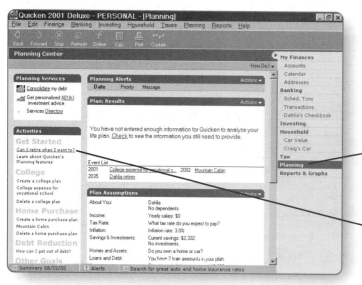

1. Click on the **Planning QuickTab**. The Planning Center will appear.

2. Click on the **Can I retire when I want to? link**. The Retirement Planner will appear in the Planning window.

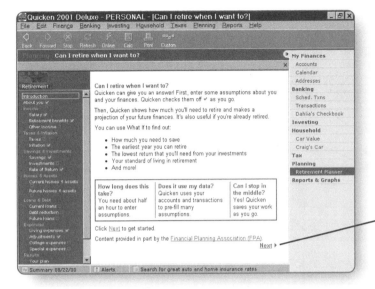

The Retirement Planner works like the other planners that you've seen used in this book, but it is much more involved. Take your time when working through the planner. There's a lot of information for you to read, and the planner will ask many questions that you will need to answer.

3. Click on the **Next link**. The next page of the planner will appear.

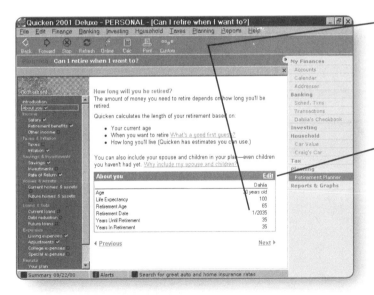

You'll notice that some areas of the planner have been filled in for you. These figures were taken from information that you entered in other areas of Quicken.

4. Click on the **Edit link** if you want to update the information. A dialog box will open, and you can change any of the information.

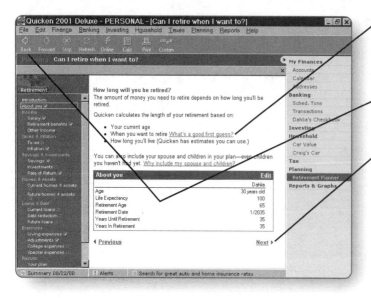

5. Click on a **link**. A page will appear that contains more information.

6. Click on **Back** to return to the page you were viewing.

7. Click on the **Next link**. The next page of the planner will appear.

TIP

If Quicken does not have enough information, you'll see a Click here link. Click on the link to open a dialog box where you can enter the needed information.

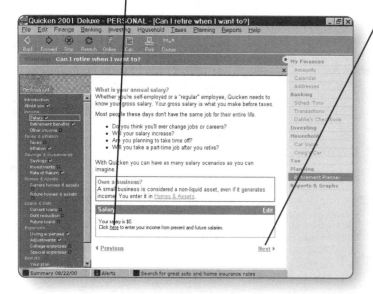

8. Click on the **Next link** and work your way through each page of the planner. When you get to the end of the planner, you'll see a Summary page. You can print this page if you want to keep a record of this version of your plan.

NOTE

You can always come back later and revise your plan. Quicken will automatically save it.

Locating a Certified Financial Planner

If you don't feel confident managing your own finances, Quicken can guide you toward some professional help. Before you begin searching for a financial planner, you may want to fill out the Financial Planner Summary form. This is a good starting point for you and your prospective financial planner.

Filling out the Financial Planner Summary

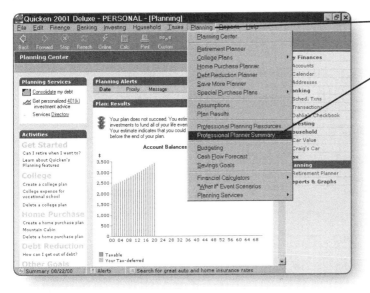

1. Click on **Planning**. The Planning menu will appear.

2. Click on **Professional Planner Summary**. The Financial Planner summary will appear in the Planning window.

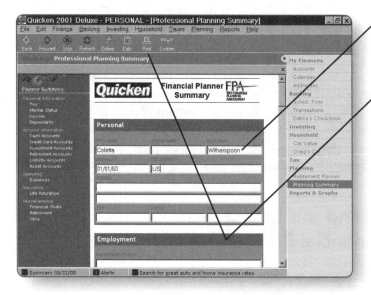

3. Click in each of the **text boxes** and **type** a **response** to the requested information.

4. Click on the **Print button** when you have completed the form. The form will print.

Searching for a Certified Financial Planner

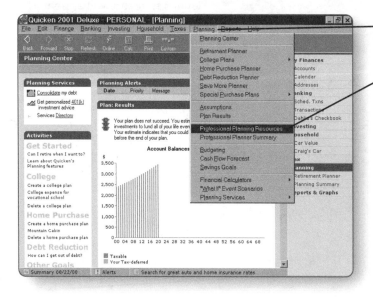

1. Click on **Planning**. The Planning menu will appear.

2. Click on **Professional Planning Resources**. The Planning Resources page will appear.

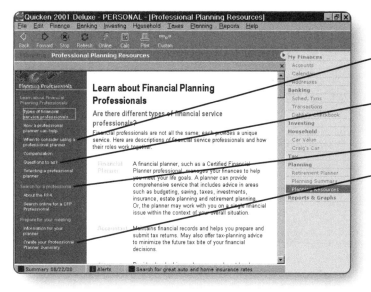

You'll find some good information at this site.

- Find some good tips on how to choose a financial planner.

- Learn how to interview a prospective financial planner.

- Search for a financial planner.

- Find out how to prepare for your first meeting with your new financial planner.

Part VI Review Questions

1. How many different calculations can you perform with the College Calculator? *See "Determining College Costs" in Chapter 20*

2. Which Quicken feature helps you start a college savings plan? *See "Using the College Planner" in Chapter 20*

3. What Web site contains information that allows you to do car comparison shopping? *See "Making Car Purchase Decisions" in Chapter 21*

4. Which Quicken tool can help you calculate car loan payments? *See "Calculating Car Loan Payments" in Chapter 21*

5. How can Quicken help you keep track of your vehicle's value and car loan? *See "Tracking Car Expenses" in Chapter 21*

6. How do you compute monthly mortgage payments on a mortgage for which you plan to apply? *See "Calculating Your Mortgage Budget" in Chapter 22*

7. What planning tool contains helpful advice about buying a home? *See "Consulting the Home Purchase Planner" in Chapter 22*

8. Where can you find competitive mortgage rates on the Web? *See "Researching Mortgage Rates on the Web" in Chapter 22*

9. Which financial calculator can help you determine how much money you'll need to save in order to have a comfortable retirement? *See "Using the Retirement Calculator" in Chapter 23*

10. Where can you find professionals who can help you manage your finances and plan for future financial needs? *See "Locating a Certified Financial Planner" in Chapter 23*

PART VII

Appendixes

A

Installing and Upgrading Quicken

Installing Quicken 2001 is a quick and easy process. Just put the CD in your computer's CD-ROM drive and the setup wizard will walk you right through the process. As you move through the installation process, you'll find that there are several Quicken components that you can install. If you have the room on your computer's hard drive, you may want to give all of the components a try. This book assumes that you are installing Quicken 2001 with all the components. This appendix will guide you through the installation and help you get Quicken 2001 on your computer.

Installing Quicken

Before you begin the installation, you need to verify that your computer meets the minimum hardware configuration, which is a 486 processor running at 66MHz with 16MB RAM. For the full installation, you need approximately 85MB of free hard disk space. You should close any programs that may be open and run Scan Disk and Disk Defragmenter before going any further.

NOTE

This appendix gives directions for installing Quicken 2001 over a previous version of Quicken. If this is the first time you are installing Quicken on a computer, not all of the steps will apply to your installation. If this is a new installation, follow the directions except for those that pertain only to the upgrade (they are noted).

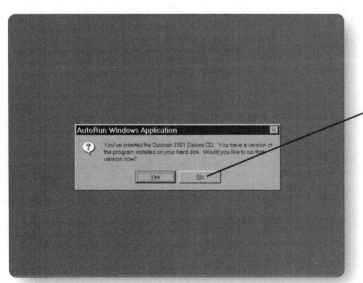

1. Place the **Quicken CD-ROM** in your computer's CD-ROM drive. The AutoRun Windows Application dialog box will open.

2. (Upgrade only) **Click** on **No**. The AutoRun Windows Application dialog box will open.

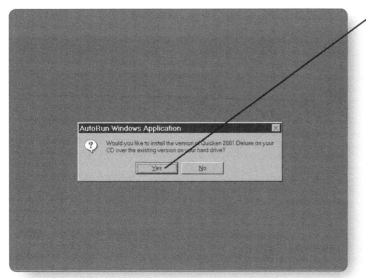

3. **Click** on **Yes**. The Quicken 2001 Deluxe Setup will begin and the Welcome screen of the setup wizard will appear.

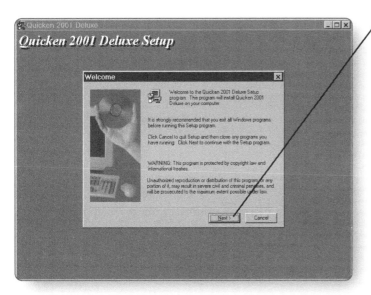

4. **Click** on **Next**. The Software License Agreement screen will appear.

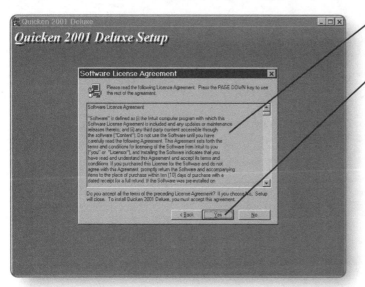

5. **Read** through the **License Agreement**.

6. **Click** on **Yes**. The Choose Destination Location screen will appear.

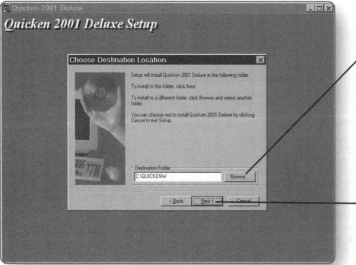

NOTE

Click on the Browse button if you want to change the destination folder. However, it is suggested that you accept the default folder.

7. **Click** on **Next**. The Confirm New Directory dialog box will open.

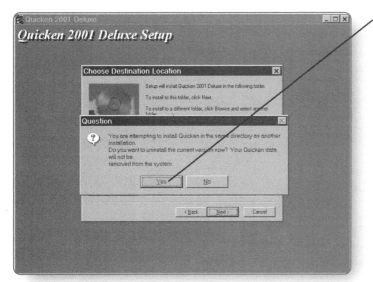

8. (Upgrade only) **Click** on **Yes**. The Confirm File Deletion dialog box will open.

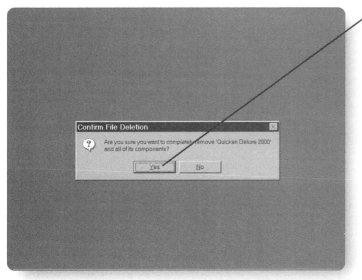

9. (Upgrade only) **Click** on **Yes**. The Remove Shared File? dialog box will open.

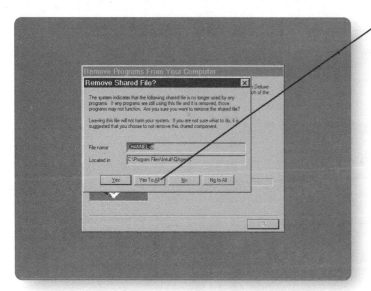

10. (Upgrade only) **Click** on **Yes To All**. The Remove Shared File? confirmation dialog box will open.

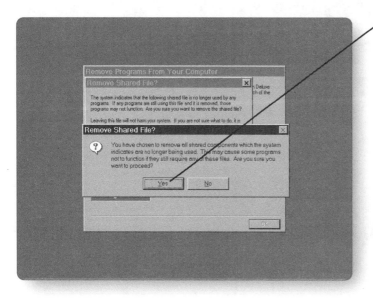

11. Click on **Yes**. The Remove Programs From Your Computer dialog box will open.

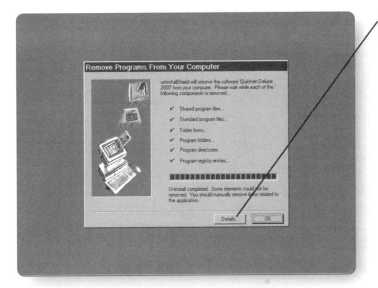

12. Click on **Details**. The Details dialog box will open.

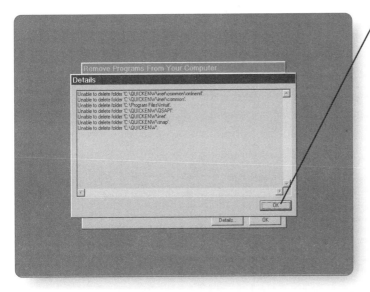

13. Click on **OK**. The Type of Installation dialog box will open.

14a. **Click** on the **Express option button** if you want to install the default Quicken components.

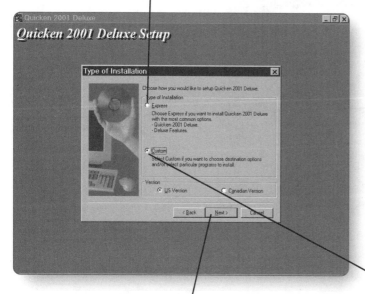

NOTE

The Express option button will not install the 128-bit SSL version of Microsoft Internet Explorer—to do online banking, you'll need a 128-bit browser, which you can install as a Custom option.

OR

14b. **Click** on the **Custom option button** if you want to select which components to install. The option will be selected.

15. **Click** on **Next**. The Select Installation Components screen will appear, if you selected the Custom option. If you selected the Express option, the program will begin installing on your system.

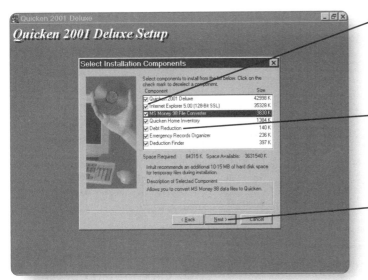

16. Click on the **Internet Explorer 5.00 (128-Bit SSL) check box** if you will be using online banking.

17. Clear any **check boxes** next to those components that you do not want to install. The check boxes will be cleared.

18. Click on **Next**. The Select Program Folder screen will appear.

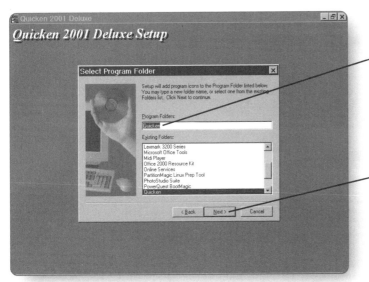

NOTE

It is suggested that you accept the default program folder where Quicken will be stored.

19. Click on **Next**. The Check Settings screen will appear.

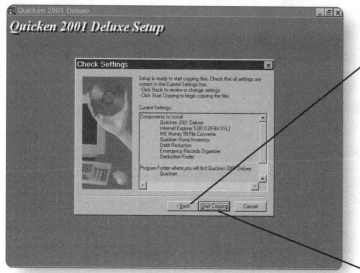

NOTE
Click on the Back button if you need to make any changes to the information displayed on this screen. Continue clicking on the Back button until you come to the page containing the setup instructions you want to change.

20. Click on **Start Copying**. The installation will begin.

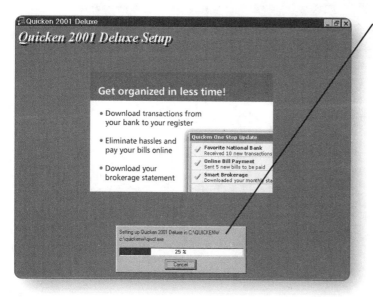

Wait while Quicken installs the software. When the setup is complete, the AOL Offer screen will appear.

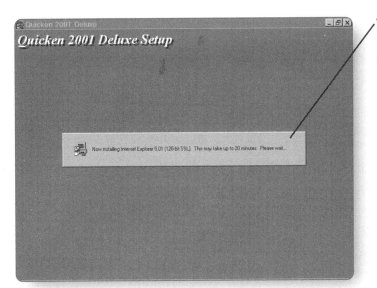

Wait while Quicken installs the 128-bit version of Microsoft Internet Explorer.

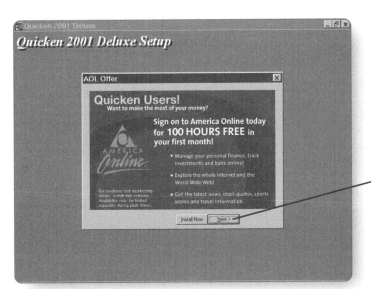

NOTE

You'll need a modem with an attached phone line before you can use the AOL offer.

21. **Click** on **Next**. The Setup Complete screen will appear.

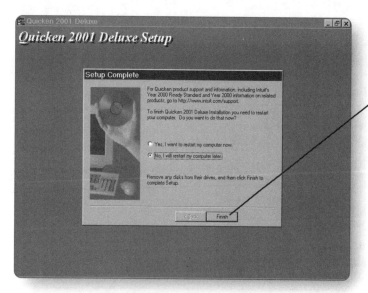

22. **Remove** the **Quicken CD-ROM** from your computer's CD-ROM drive.

23. **Click** on **Finish**. Your computer will restart and the Quicken program will finish the installation process.

B

Using Shortcut Keys with Quicken

You may have noticed the keyboard shortcuts listed on the right side of the Quicken menus. You can use these shortcuts to execute commands without using the mouse to open the menus. Not only do these shortcuts speed up your productivity, but they also help decrease wrist strain caused by excessive mouse usage. Keep these shortcut guides close at hand and practice using these keyboard shortcuts. You'll find that with a little time, you'll be using the keyboard as naturally as you once used the mouse. In this appendix, you'll learn how to use shortcut keys to:

- Move around the Quicken window
- Work with the registers
- Use the Financial Calendar and budgets

Moving around Quicken

The following table shows you some common keyboard shortcuts to use when navigating between open windows that you have been viewing in Quicken.

Working with Quicken Files

To execute this command	Do this
Move backward between previously displayed windows	Press the Alt and Left Arrow keys simultaneously (Alt+Left Arrow)
Move forward between previously displayed windows	Press Alt+Right Arrow
Display the Quicken Home Page	Press Alt+Home
Print the page you are viewing	Press Ctrl+P
Get Help on the window you are viewing	Press F1

It's easy to open and back up any data files with these shortcuts.

To execute this command	Do this
Open a new data file	Press the Ctrl and O keys simultaneously (Ctrl+O)
Back up a data file	Press Ctrl+B

Using the Register

You'll probably spend most of your time in Quicken working with the various account registers. Here are a few simple keyboard shortcuts you can use while you're working in any of them.

Navigating the Register

To execute this command	Do this
Open the register	Press the Ctrl and R keys simultaneously (Ctrl+R)
Go to the first transaction in a register	Press Ctrl+Home
Move to the last transaction in a register	Press Ctrl+End
Go to the first field in a transaction	Press Home twice
Go to the last field in a transaction	Press End twice
Move to the next field or column	Press Tab
Move to the previous field or column	Press Shift+Tab
Go to the beginning of a field	Press Home
Go to the end of a field	Press End
Move to the next transaction	Press Down Arrow
Move to the previous transaction	Press Up Arrow

Entering Transactions in the Register

To execute this command	Do this
Select an account	Press Ctrl+A
Go to a new transaction	Press Ctrl+N
Enter a transaction	Press Enter
Open the Split Transaction window	Press Ctrl+S
Close the Split Transaction window	Press Ctrl+Enter
Pay a scheduled transaction	Press Ctrl+J
Memorize a transaction	Press Ctrl+M
Recall a memorized transaction	Press Ctrl+T

Editing Transactions in the Register

To execute this command	Do this
Decrease the selected date or check number	Press – (Minus key)
Increase the selected date or check number	Press + (Plus key)
Find a transaction	Press Ctrl+F
Cut a field in the register	Press Shift+Del
Copy a field in the register	Press Ctrl+Ins
Paste a field in the register	Press Shift+Ins
Delete a transaction	Press Ctrl+D
Void a transaction	Press Alt+D

Working with Planning Tools

Two common planning tools are the Financial Calendar and the Budget. It's possible to maneuver your way through these tools without the aid of a mouse.

Moving around the Financial Calendar

To execute this command	Do this
Open the Financial Calendar	Press Ctrl+K
Select the current date	Press T
Go to the first day of the current month	Press M
Go to the last day of the current month	Press H
Display the first day of the current year	Press Y
Display the last day of the current year	Press R
Go to a specific date	Press Alt+G
Add a note to the calendar	Press Alt+N

Creating a Budget

To execute this command	Do this
Go to the first row in the budget	Press the Ctrl and Home keys simultaneously (Ctrl+Home)
Go to the last row in the budget	Press Ctrl+End
Move to the right in a row of budget items	Press Tab
Move to the left in a row of budget items	Press Shift+Tab
Go to the row above the currently selected row	Press Up Arrow
Go to the row below the currently selected row	Press Down Arrow
Go to the first cell in the current row	Press Home+Home
Go to the last cell in the current row	Press End+End
Scroll the budget one page to the left	Press Ctrl+Left Arrow
Scroll the budget one page to the right	Press Ctrl+Right Arrow
Scroll up the budget to display the previous group of categories	Press Page Up
Scroll down the budget to display the next group of categories	Press Page Down
Undo the last amount entered	Press Esc

Glossary

A

Accounts. Quicken organizes your financial information into separate categories that resemble your real-world accounts for your assets and liabilities. Using these accounts, you can track your checking and savings activities, your mortgage and credit card transactions, and all of your other financial activities.

Accounts list. This is Quicken's overview of your accounts.

Accrual-basis accounting. This is an accounting method that recognizes obligations when they occur and income when the customer is billed.

Adjustable rate loans. These are loans with a variable interest rate. When the interest rate of your adjustable rate loan changes, Quicken can calculate your new payment amount using the new interest rate.

Amortize. To write off a regular part of an asset's cost over a specified time period.

Asset. An item that you own: your car, real estate, investments, and so on. A business definition of an asset is something that has a probable future economic benefit, is controlled by the business, and came about from a prior transaction or event.

Asset depreciation range. This is the defined range of depreciable (amortizable) lives allowed by the Internal Revenue Service for each class of asset. This was replaced by the Accelerated Cost Recovery System (ACRS) but was later revived in the 1986 Tax Reform Act and is used to determine class lives.

B

Balance. The difference between total debits and total credits to an account, as in loan balance or bank balance.

Balloon payment. The last payment on a loan if it is significantly larger than previous payments. These kinds of loans are also called partially amortized loans.

Billminder. A list of upcoming financial actions, bills to pay, payment instructions, and so on.

Blue Chip. A high-quality common stock with a long history of consistently paying dividends. These are attractive long-term investments.

Budget. A plan of actions and programs expressed in assets, liabilities, revenue, and expenses that directs financial planning and activities to meet the requirements for obtaining a specific operational objective.

C

Cash flow. This is the net result of cash receipts less cash disbursements for a particular operation or asset over a specified period of time.

Categories. A method of identifying transactions by placing them in related groups. An example would be an income category to keep track of deposits and an expense category for automotive repair costs.

Classes. Quicken identifies transactions by assigning them to classes based upon details supplied by you specifying where, when, to whom, and to what the transactions apply.

Credit. (1) The entry made in the right-hand column of an account. In double-entry bookkeeping, credits are an increase in the liabilities, equity, and revenue accounts, but they are a decrease in the asset and expense accounts. (2) The ability to borrow money or buy things with a promise to pay later.

Credit analysis. A process used to determine the suitability of a potential creditor to receive credit and how much credit should be given.

D

Debit. The bookkeeping entry made on the left side of the account. In double-entry bookkeeping, a debit is an increase in the asset and expense accounts and a decrease in the liabilities, equity, and revenue accounts.

Demand deposit. This is an account where funds may be withdrawn, or transferred on demand to another person, by means of a check. A checking account is an example of a demand account.

Disposable income. This is your income less income tax and all other government deductions. Disposable income is what most people think of as their take-home pay.

Dividend. Money paid to shareholders of a money market fund, a stock, or a mutual fund.

E

Embezzlement. The theft of money or property from a business by a person responsible for its safekeeping.

Encumbrance. A lien on assets used to secure a loan.

Ending balance. The balance of all transactions in the account register.

Exchange rate. The ratio at which one currency or commodity can be exchanged for another.

Excise tax. This is a tax levied on specific goods or services to collect money for a specified purpose. The excise tax on gasoline is an example—the money is used to build and maintain the road system.

Expenditure. A payment made with cash or property (or a promise to pay later) to obtain an asset or a service.

Expense. Something paid out to obtain revenue in the current period. One example is the depletion of an asset through depreciation. Another example is to incur an obligation to which regular payments are made, such as in an equipment lease.

F

Factoring. The sale of a firm's accounts receivable at a discount and without recourse to avoid having to wait until the accounts mature, or to avoid collection costs.

Financial statement. A report containing a snapshot financial representation of the organization. It usually contains a balance sheet, an income statement, and a statement of changes in financial condition.

Fixed asset. An asset, purchased for the use of the organization and not intended for resale, with a life of more than one year. Property, plant, and equipment are first considerations.

Fixed cost. Costs that remain constant as expenses regardless of changes in operation. Rent, insurance, and licensing are examples of fixed-cost expenses.

G

General partner. The partner who is liable for all debts and obligations incurred by the partnership.

Graph. A visual representation of data, such as a pie chart or bar chart that might represent the distribution of your salary.

Gross income. The amount of money received from the sale of goods or services less the cost of those goods or services. Gross income less the operating expenses of the company is called net income.

Gross sales. This is the total of all sales before the adjustment for returns and discounts. It is the total number of units sold multiplied by the unit sales price.

Growth stock. This is a group name applied to companies that have no earnings record from past operations. The value of the company is based on speculation about future earnings. These stocks may have a potential for high return because they do have a faster than usual rise in the market and industry. Because they are speculative in nature and the expected gains may not materialize at all, growth stocks have a high risk associated with them.

H

Hidden accounts. These are accounts that Quicken uses to keep track of accounts that are obsolete or have a zero balance. By hiding accounts, you can remove an account and its balance from your list of accounts but still retain the transaction information.

I

Income. This is money earned during a specific period that increases total assets. This can come from salaries, rent, interest earned, gifts, commissions, and so on. Any excess over expense is called net income.

Individual Retirement Account (IRA). A special account for the investment of money for retirement that meets the government regulations for an account that does not generate any taxable income as long as the funds remain in the account.

J

Joint stock company. A group of individuals joined together to form and operate a business. Similar to a corporation except that the investors are not given limited liability.

Joint tenancy. An arrangement in which property or real estate is deeded and held by two or more persons who hold an undivided interest in the property. Should one of the members die, the property will revert to the control of the remaining member(s) without the need to go through the estate of the deceased.

K

Keogh plan. A retirement plan for self-employed persons who meet certain requirements. A Keogh plan member may make an annual contribution up to 25% of income or a maximum amount of $30,000.

Kiting. The illegal practice of concealing a cash shortage by taking advantage of the time that it takes for a check to clear through the banking system.

L

Lead time. This is the number of business days from the time you send online payment instructions until the payment is received by the payee. Quicken automatically calculates this number when you enter payment instructions.

Liability. An amount payable in dollars or services. The party having the liability is called a debtor.

Lien. The right of a second party to take control over or possession of the property of another to satisfy a debt or duty obligation.

M

Maturity date. The date by which the principal of a debt must be paid.

N

Net worth. Total assets minus total liabilities. This represents an individual's personal equity; in a business, this would be the shareholders' equity.

Nonprofit organization. An organization that meets a need for goods and services that is structured so that no one involved in the organization may benefit from or share in the profits or losses. These organizations are exempt from taxes, and donations to them are tax deductible.

Nontaxable gross income. Money received by a taxpayer that is not taxed, like a gift.

O

Operating loss. The amount of money by which the business's operating expenses added to the cost of goods sold exceeds the operating revenue.

Operating revenue. Net sales plus all other regular business income.

Operating risk. The risk encountered because of a fluctuating operating revenue stream. The higher the risk, the more unstable the company.

Owner's equity. The owner's interest in the assets of the business. These are represented by capital contributions and retained earnings.

P

Paid-in capital. The results of donations to the company or sale of treasury or capital stock at a price above par value.

Par value. The arbitrary value assigned to one share of stock by the company charter. This is the amount printed on the certificate.

Patent. An exclusive right to manufacture and market a product or a process for 17 years without interference or infringement. Patents are issued by the government to companies and individuals.

Q

Quicken. Personal finance software by Intuit, Inc.

QuickTabs. A Quicken feature that keeps the most-used windows open and provides tabs at the right of the screen to facilitate switching back and forth from one window to another one.

Quickzoom. A Quicken feature that enables you to get a detailed display of a graph or report.

Quoted price. The last transaction price of a commodity or a listed security.

R

Recession. A downturn in the economy as indicated by a drop in the gross national product.

Reconcile window. This window displays cleared transactions that occur before the statement end date for reconciling an online account to a statement.

Reconciliation. Ensuring that there is agreement between your account register and the statements you receive from financial institutions.

Retirement accounts. Accounts in which the income generated by the deposits does not incur a tax liability as long as it remains in the account.

S

Short-term debt. Money owed to a creditor with a repayment term of less than one year.

Shrinkage. The difference between inventory on the books and the actual inventory on hand.

Simple interest. Interest that is based on the original principal and is not compounded.

Speculation. The method of investment that puts money in high-risk investments to increase the chance of higher capital gain.

Stock quotes. Continuously updated prices of stocks and securities. Quicken provides access to these prices through Internet access.

T

Tax credit. A reduction in taxes payable where the basis for reducing the taxpayer's obligation is dollar for dollar for the amount of the credit.

Transaction. Any action or item that affects the balance of an account, including checks, fees, service charges, deposits, and so on.

Treasury bill (T bill). An actively marketed, low-risk short-term obligation of the government. These are sold without interest at a discount and are redeemed in 91 or 182 days at face value. Occasionally, there are some T bills that are sold for nine or 12 months. T bill amounts range from $10,000 to $1,000,000.

Treasury bond. (1) A long-term obligation of the federal government with maturities of 10 years or more that is sold in minimum amounts of $1,000. (2) A long-term obligation sold by a corporation and then repurchased (retired) by the corporation at a later date.

Treasury certificate. A debt security of the federal government bearing coupon interest, with a maturity date of one year or less.

Treasury notes. Actively marketed obligations of the federal government with maturities of one to 10 years.

U

Unappropriated retained earnings. Funds in the retained earnings account that are available for disbursement as dividends.

Unaudited statement. A statement that was not prepared by an accountant according to the Generally Accepted Auditing Standards (GAAP).

Unit trust. A mutual fund whose only investments are in bonds.

Unlimited liability. The liability that applies to owners of sole proprietorships or general partnerships. Shareholders in corporations have limited liability, which limits their risk of loss to the investment they made in the stock.

V

Variable annuity. An investment through an investment or insurance company in which the periodic annuity payments are dependent on the performance of the portfolio.

Variable costs. These are costs that vary in direct proportion to changes in activity. Examples are vehicle operation expenses or the costs of overtime hours.

Venture capital. A potential funding source for new or restructured businesses where the potential for high return is great, but so is the risk. Often, wealthy individual investors or investment clubs and small investment companies participate in venture capital because of the big potential for return.

Vested. A description of an employee's paid-up rights to retirement benefits. These are benefits not contingent on the employee's remaining in the employ of the organization.

Voucher check. A business check with additional voucher space on the side to allow for more detail about the transaction.

Vouching. The recognition of obligations and the authorization of cash disbursements.

W

Warranty. The agreement of a seller or manufacturer to settle any grievances over the quality or performance of an item for a specified amount of time.

Windfall profits. Unexpected unearned income not usually a result of the investment or effort of the person benefiting.

Worker's compensation. A program of compensation to a worker injured on the job, made without consideration for negligence.

Index